Seasons of Salt

Seasons of Salt

Meditations

Spread through the seasons
Sprinkled with the salt
Of humor and heartbreak,
Wisdom, faith, and love

Millie Horlacher

iUniverse, Inc.
New York   Bloomington

Seasons of Salt
Meditations

Copyright © 2009 Millie Horlacher

Cover and author photos by Jeff Horlacher

Scripture quotations and references are from the New Revised Standard Version of the Bible, copyright 1989, Division of Christian Education of the National Council of the Churches of Christ in the United States of America. Used by permission. All rights reserved.

iUniverse books may be ordered through booksellers or by contacting:

iUniverse
1663 Liberty Drive
Bloomington, IN 47403
www.iuniverse.com
1-800-Authors (1-800-288-4677)

ISBN: 978-1-4401-6166-7 (pbk)
ISBN: 978-1-4401-6167-4 (cloth)
ISBN: 978-1-4401-6168-1 (ebook)

Printed in the United States of America

iUniverse rev. date: 8/27/09

Let your speech always be gracious, seasoned with salt, so that you may know how you ought to answer everyone.

—Colossians 4:6

Dedicated to my husband Wayne, to our children Jeff, Jan, and Jim, and to the memory of our daughter Joan, who added spice and spirit to the lives of our family and of all those who knew her.

Contents

List of Scripture Readings

Acknowledgments

Special thanks to my editor Karen Sells Brown; to my pastors through the years; to the Colby Writers Group for their patient support; to my many faith sisters of the United Methodist Women who encouraged me to write this book; to those many friends and family who listened and read, counseled and corrected as they traveled with me on this publishing journey; and to the many writers before me who have shared their faith through their words.

Advance Praise for Seasons of Salt

"Engaging! Enchanting! Excellent! This collection of anecdotal devotions is based on the author's experiences of subjects as disparate as a banquet, a nail, and weevils. Millie Horlacher draws the reader into the narrative, then gently shares insights and applications to daily life. Each closing prayer is a mini-masterpiece, leading seekers to a deeper commitment to the call of Christ. A must-read!"

—JoEva McClellan,
past President, Kansas West Conference,
United Methodist Women

"These moving devotions by Millie Horlacher reflect who she is as a person: a deeply committed Christian, an advocate for justice, a compassionate friend, and a courageous woman in the face of personal loss and pain."

—Bishop Fritz and Etta Mae Mutti

"Millie's writing exemplifies her faithful Christian witness and delightful attitude. Relating to real-life experiences can give great insight into God's awesome power, and I know you will enjoy this collection of inspiring stories!"

—Dixie Brewster,
Kansas West Conference,
United Methodist Church

Foreword

As the clock crept closer to dismissal time, we squirmed in anticipation and shuffled our feet under our desks. The older boys whispered plans for a race after school. The upper-grade girls giggled softly. Miss Virginia rapped on her teacher's desk for quiet, with limited response. Picking up a large straight pin, she told us that as soon as we could hear the pin hit the floor when she dropped it behind the upright piano, school would be dismissed. Our feet suddenly became still and silent. The whispering and giggling stopped. We held our breath as we strained to hear the faint sound of the pin on the hardwood floor. There. We heard it!

And from this childhood memory of a school experience, Millie Horlacher begins to gently guide us in listening for God. She evokes a rich spirituality rooted in the chaos and uncertainty of everyday life.

Every season, cold or warm, challenging or business-as-usual, makes new demands on us. Each season brings experiences, understandings, and insights. Millie Horlacher's book of meditations allows us to take a moment for quiet reflection and to discover the promise of new beginnings and new journeys full of hope and joy. Through the ordinary context of her life, she helps us to look deeper and closer into our own lives—to find peace, faith, and encouragement.

Rev. James Mardock
Pastor, Colby United Methodist Church

Preface

Salt Not Sugar

"You are the salt of the earth; but if the salt has lost its taste, how can its saltiness be restored? It is no longer good for anything, but is thrown out and trampled underfoot."
—Matthew 5:13

In this book, I offer you a collection of meditations to use in your private devotional times or for group devotions. The underlying message in every meditation is that God is with us in our everyday lives as well as in our moments of grief and in our times of celebration. Each meditation begins with a Scripture reading, then relates life experience to the Biblical message, and ends with prayer. The list of Scripture readings will help you locate a meditation related to a particular Bible passage. The meditations are grouped into thematic sections, so you may wish to begin with the section that interests you most or with the current liturgical season in the section "Traveling Through the Christian Year," which includes highlights of the church calendar. Come with me as we undertake a spiritual journey together.

These meditations are what I have come to call "salty." Such meditations can help us to center our thoughts on Scripture, to listen for and to hear the voice of the Holy

Spirit. The following glimpse into my personal life illustrates what I mean by salty meditations.

Throughout our house, we keep jars and tins filled with candy. My husband is one of those rare people who can eat generous amounts of candy without suffering weight gain or other ill effects. Although my consumption of sweets is considerably less, my weight gain is considerably more. I am good at gaining weight. I am also good at rationalizing. Several years ago a candy company distributed candy orange slices that incorporated vitamin C. I was delighted. Just three soft, chewy slices supplied the daily requirement of vitamin C. No animal fat, no cholesterol, only a few calories, a little sugar, a burst of quick energy, and that vitamin C. Wonderful! I could carry my vitamin C in my purse—and rationalize all the way to the dentist.

While orange slices may not be your favorite candy, most of us do like sweets. We rationalize the side effects as we eat "just a bite" of a brownie or a piece of candy. In our busy lives, many of us also rationalize about our choice of meditations. We select "short and sweet" devotions, feel-good poems, and easy-to-sing choruses that have little actual meaning. Sometimes we intentionally "lighten up" a deep meditation. Lighter devotional fare may be appropriate at times; in the midst of severe pain, illness, deep fatigue, or unusual stress, something light might be all we can digest. Even then, we may find such devotions leave us hungering for some real spiritual food. Superficial devotions given only to fill a slot on the program or a few minutes of personal devotional time have lost their saltiness. Just as the burst of energy from sugar-laden candy is short-lived, so are the benefits of "sugary" devotions.

In Matthew 5:13, Jesus told the disciples that they were the salt of the earth. They, and we, are to be the grains of salt in the world, neither isolated from the world nor compromised by the world. The disciples were to keep the message pure, to preserve it, and to spread it throughout the world. Salt becomes impure when it is mixed with too many other elements and loses its effectiveness. Jesus wanted the disciples to remain pure and focused on their mission to the world—to not lose their "saltiness."

This metaphor has many layers of meaning. *Salt*, in the Bible, could mean sacrifice, covenant, or fidelity. Eating together was called "sharing the salt," which expressed a binding relationship. *Salt* also meant purification. It was a seasoning and a preservative. Today, as then, salt enhances the flavor of food. Salty meditations share many of these same traits. Salty meditations recognize the possibility of sacrifice and call for faith and fidelity, purity and patience. Such meditations can challenge, strengthen, and encourage those who read or hear them. Salty meditations enhance the flavor of our lives with spiritual food that endures.

These meditations are taken from the salt-sprinkled seasons of my life, including my personal experiences of deep grief and pain as well as times of great joy and laughter. They are the fruit of my long experience of hearing and giving devotions. Years of guidance and leadership, changes and challenges, study and fellowship with other Christians are reflected in the meditations. Although my bookshelves are filled with well-worn Bible commentaries and dictionaries, study guides, and devotional books, I am not a scholar. I am a student whose education is not complete. I have questions yet unanswered. Undoubtedly, I would write some of these meditations differently in the future, and some might bring me to ask myself, "Where did I get *that*?" My understanding of the Scriptures is constantly evolving.

Each time we read the Scriptures, we open the potential for new dimensions of God's word to be revealed to us. Please take time for the Scripture reading at the beginning of each meditation. Even if you have memorized the verses, you may be surprised at the sudden impact a word or phrase will have on your interpretation of the passage. In these meditations, I refer to the New Revised Standard Version of the Bible, although my shelf holds many different versions and translations. Your favorite version may give you a different understanding of the text. Explore other translations of Scripture for deeper insights. Keep your heart and mind open to the unexpected.

Prayerfully read these meditations; enjoy and ponder, agree or disagree. Travel with me through our common experiences of family, food, childhood games, through our shared identity as children of God, and finally through the calendar of the Christian year. Just as a small amount of salt sprinkled into a pot of soup spreads throughout the whole pot, our grains of salt can spread the message of Christ to those around us. May you and I never lose our saltiness.

Thank you for joining me in this journey of Christian discipleship.

God be with you,
Millie Horlacher

Part 1

All in the Family

Tumbled through time, tossed and tested, the family has survived. In all cultures, in grand or gross configurations, our families shape and mold us. Family ties stretch across the miles and years. They tug at us when we fix the turkey for Thanksgiving or hang the lights at Christmas. We feel the pull when we see Grandpa's sly little wink in a grandchild. Families are where we live. Faith is formed and nurtured in families. Love is grown or ground down. And in families, the sacred can emerge in unexpected places and events.

Identity

Read Romans 8:14–17.

With my new thick pencils and Big Chief tablet placed just so on my desk in front of me, I watched intently as our teacher pulled down a wonderful map mounted like a window shade on the wall at the front of the room. She pointed out where we lived: the Northern Hemisphere, the North American continent, the United States, and finally, our very own state of Kansas. Best of all, she traced that squiggly line in the northeast corner of Kansas and our own Atchison County. Eyes wide with wonder and referring frequently to the map, I printed slowly and carefully in large block letters my name and address on the front of my new tablet:

> Mildred Evelyn Hundley
> Route 1
> Horton, Kansas
> United States
> North America
> Northern Hemisphere
> The World

The words filled the entire tablet cover and added detail to the image of the Indian chief.

I was at a specific spot on that map and on the globe on the teacher's desk. It was thrilling to me. Each of us in that room, big and little, each child at each desk belonged to a specific place on that huge map. Wow!

I had another sense of place. I had a place in my family. I was part of a large extended family of parents and grandparents, brothers and sisters, cousins, aunts and uncles. After an evening of help from my mother, the next morning I wrote on the very back of my tablet: Mildred Evelyn Hundley, followed by the names of my parents, my paternal grandparents, and my maternal grandparents.

The teacher was proud of my sense of identity. I decided to surprise her. My maternal grandfather had only gone as far as second grade, but he had gone to the same country school I now attended. He had even scratched his name on his desk. Now, decades later, I sat in the same desk. Varnishing and scrubbing had reduced his scratched signature to just a faint indentation on the desk, but it was my grandpa's name. At recess, I asked my oldest brother to lend me his metal compass. Then I very carefully scratched my name beneath Grandpa's name.

The teacher did not appreciate the historical significance. She must have appreciated my sense of identity with my family, as I do not recall being punished other than a verbal scolding. My scratched signature was faint, and the first polishing of the desk erased my effort at recording history.

As an adult, I have written my name countless times. I have changed my residential address. As a shy college student, I became known as "Millie" rather than "Mildred." When I married, I changed my surname.

When I was baptized, my name was added to a new genealogical chart. I became a member of Christ's family. Each baptized person is my sister or brother in the adopted family of God. I might never have known my birth parents. I could be a foster child, a runaway child, a stepchild; yet beyond any of those conditions, I am an adopted daughter of God. That new relationship is my most basic identity. It will never change regardless of marriages or moves or new social groups. These became the final lines of my family identity and address:

> A Sister in Christ
> Daughter of God
> Granddaughter of Abraham
> Living in God's World

My extended biological family has grown so large that at family reunions we often wear nametags identifying our place on the family tree. My faith family is also huge. My faith family tree has many branches. I am a member of the United Methodist branch of the Christian family tree. My Christian brothers and sisters are everywhere. Do they recognize me? Do I recognize them?

Prayer: Dear God, our Holy Parent, thank you for our adoption. Grant us the courage and strength to be worthy members of your family. Give us eyes to recognize our brothers and sisters in Christ even when our differences disguise our identities. Help us to give and receive the love and support only such a family can give. Amen.

Enabled to Love

Read 1 John 4:7–12.

It was midnight. Two thin brothers, seven and nine years old, shivered in the night coolness as they stood beside the judge who had brought them to our home. Their feet were clad in shoes that were too big. Cut-off jeans completed their outfits. The two brothers were the first of our foster children. Given a snack and tucked into clean, warm beds for the first time in weeks, they quickly drifted off to sleep. This new bedroom was a far cry from the garages they had crept into under cover of darkness to find shelter from the night.

We were amazed at the survival skills of these children. They knew how to steal food from grocery stores and candy from vending machines, and how to slip into the swimming pool for a refreshing swim, wearing those same cut-off jeans as swimsuits. Our glimpse into their world opened up to us the desperate needs of children even in our small, snug community.

Child neglect and abuse are known all too well by teachers, pastors, social workers, the courts, and law enforcement. Many of us are only dimly aware of the extent of the problems of the children and families in our communities. Much abuse is hidden, for it happens in all social and economic levels. It even happens within families who sit in our pews.

Our journey into that crying world was full of sorrow and joy, of apparent success and probable failure. Our foster children ranged in age from two days to sixteen years. The children were with us from a few days to almost a year. Our task was to provide emergency and interim care as courts and social workers attempted to make the best decisions for the children. We could not adopt any of them because of the rules at that time.

"Don't get too attached. You will have to give them up at some point." That was the advice given us. We found that advice impossible to follow. In our view, attachment was exactly what these children needed. We loved the children from the time they were brought to our front door. From the tiny two-day-old infant to the teenage unwed mother relinquishing her baby for adoption, we loved them wholeheartedly and did, indeed, become attached to them. We grieved for each one when they left us.

Some of the children clung to us as our tears mingled with their tears. Some stood on the driveway with a paper sack of belongings in hand, shoulders slumped and eyes averted, awaiting the social worker and yet another home. One little boy was sent to his new home with prayers from his adoptive mother and from us. Unfortunately, that little boy soon found himself once again in a broken home. "Our" baby eventually found an excellent adoptive home, and his new parents kept in contact with us for a few months. We sometimes sat on courthouse benches with frightened children as the rights of their biological parents were legally severed. Because of the circumstances at the time of our foster parenting, we generally did not know what became of the children.

We also are adopted. We are the adopted children of Abraham. We are loved wholeheartedly. Our earthly families might be circles of love or they might be shattered and shameful. But all of us have another family that embraces us as no other could.

Some of our foster children enjoyed numerous soaks in the bathtub before the gray of their unwashed bodies disappeared. So too, our spirits require numerous soaks of grace to cleanse our souls. We may come to God bruised and broken. We may be blind to the needs of others. We are often selfish, and yet we come to God knowing that God loves and accepts us and expects us to grow into the fullness of humanity as expressed by Christ. We are enabled to love others knowing that we are beloved by God. By showing love to our foster children, we hope that we enabled them to express and accept love later in their lives.

Prayer: Holy Parent, grant us the eyes to see and ears to hear the cries of the world. Give us strong hearts and hands to wipe away the tears and to give love as we receive your love. Guide us in ways that reduce suffering and produce justice for the least of these, your children. Amen.

Chores

Read Psalm 46:1–3.

When I was a child, my vivid imagination made routine chores a test of my courage. Every afternoon I filled the empty coal buckets from the piles of coal stored in the space under the kitchen and back porch. Even as a teenager, I dreaded going to that space. After the long bus ride home from school in winter, chores were often done in the early evening darkness. The short distance from the back door to the coal bin was well lit, but once in the bin, there was only murky light at best. The buckets were filled partly by sight and partly by feel. I had never encountered so much as a mouse in the mounds of coal, but some wild animal *might* have managed to slip under the door, a skunk *might* have been wintering in the corner. Who knew what lingered in the darkness?

Getting coal was not my only frightening childhood task; another daunting chore was getting potatoes from the potato cave. Abundant crops of potatoes were stored in a stone-walled cave some distance from the house. Bull and black snakes found the constant temperature of the cave to their liking and lived year round in the walls. The snakes were harmless and served as effective controls for rats and mice. Nevertheless, I was afraid of them and dreaded filling the potato bucket. A garden hoe was as important a part of my equipment for getting potatoes as that potato bucket.

Neither of these chores carried any actual risk to me. My childish imagination did its own work quite well in raising my heart rate.

Fortunately, in Sunday school classes and from my parents, I had learned many Bible verses and hymns. I was able to complete my chores by saying over and over to myself, "God will take care of me, and God will take care of me." That assurance carried me through many a frightening childhood experience.

Maturity does not automatically guarantee relief from unrealistic fear. As parents, we may have difficulty putting aside the "what-might-happens" when our children venture out our front doors and away from our presence and protection.

As adults, we face the knowledge that the future is always murky, that our long-range plans must be written in pencil. Like that potato cave filled with harmless snakes, life means encountering new ideas, facing our doubts, and feeling our way through inevitable snares. Realistically evaluating dangers, taking reasonable precautions, and most of all knowing that God is our refuge and strength will enable us to live life at its fullest, free from childish fears.

I know that God is with me, in my daily life as well as in crises. Though I no longer fill coal buckets or get potatoes from a cave with snakes, I still have situations when I say to myself, "God will take care of me."

And God does, sometimes with a garden hoe.

Prayer: God of refuge and strength, we come to you with our real and imagined fears. Enfold us in your arms. Protect and strengthen us in our daily lives. Calm our swirling imaginations, and give us peace. Amen.

Everybody Needs a Bath

Read 1 John 1: 5–10.

Decades ago, our family's Saturday night baths took considerable preparation. In my role as big sister, I carried the washtub from the back porch and put it close to the dining room stove for my younger siblings' baths. I filled a milk bucket with hot water from the reservoir at the end of the kitchen stove and carefully poured the water into the washtub. Towels arranged on the backs of chairs surrounding the tub provided a sense of privacy and shielded the area from drafts. We older and more modest children moved the washtub to a bedroom. Summer baths were sometimes taken on the back sidewalk in the moonlight. Regardless of the season, the younger children were subjected to post-bath inspections to assure that their ears and necks really were clean.

Bathing customs have changed over the centuries and vary greatly in different cultures. We might laugh or shudder at the bathing practices of people long ago or far away. The people in Hellenistic times cleansed themselves in elaborate baths constructed in palaces and gyms. The Romans brought their practice of bathing to Britain, and the public baths in Bath, England, were built. In Europe during the Middle Ages, everyone in the family used the same water to bathe. May was the favored month for their annual baths. The male head of the family bathed first, then down the line according to age, with the babies bathed last. By then the bath water was quite muddied. The expression "Don't throw the baby out with the bath water" came from that period. In regions of the world with warm climates and abundant water, frequent or even daily baths were common.

Today many people face enormous challenges in maintaining personal cleanliness. Refugees, the poor, and residents of drought-stricken areas may have to hunt daily for minimal amounts of drinking water. The fortunate few of us in the world with adequate water supplies have no excuse for neglecting our personal hygiene and endangering our health. We have learned that even when our hands appear clean, unseen bacteria thrive on unwashed hands. Teachers and preachers, farmers and truck drivers, athletes dripping with perspiration and workers sitting at desks in air-conditioned offices, all need baths. Everybody needs a bath.

In the Bible, we read that the Jews bathed for personal cleanliness, for showing hospitality to guests, and, most important, for ritual purification. Public baths were features of health resorts at the hot springs in Galilee and Calirrhoe. The pool of Bethesda mentioned in the New Testament was a public bath. John the Baptist baptized Jesus in the Jordan River.

In our baptismal rites, water is a powerful symbol

of repentance, rebirth, and the washing away of sin. As Christians, we know that everyone needs a spiritual bath. The writer of 1 John emphasized the need for each one of us to be cleansed by Jesus. Each of us needs forgiveness for his or her sins, whether those sins are visible to others or not. Even when we appear clean, we know our sins all too well. Just as our parents could see the unwashed body parts of their protesting children, God can see our sin.

We need a bath. We scrub with soap. We soak in scalding water. Yet the smudges of our failed reformations remain. Finally, with glistening eyes or racking sobs, we shed tears of repentance. We humbly bow before God, and the cleansing bath of our faithful and just God leaves us truly clean.

Prayer: Forgiving, faithful, and just God, wash us now; cleanse us of all deceit and wickedness. We do things we know are wrong and fail to do things we know are right. Help us to have the courage and strength to act on what we profess. Forgive us for our many failings. Wrap us in your love that we might grow in a grace-full life. Amen.

Through a Paper Narrowly

Read Matthew 7:13–14.

Our son rolled his worship bulletin into a cylinder and focused it on the pulpit. He studied the pastor and then scanned the choir. His youngest sister followed suit. Because she was shorter, her view through the paper tube was different from her brother's. I could see an argument brewing and attempted to get the attention of their father, who was temporarily "resting" his eyes. This was not my best worship service experience.

Nor was it really something to get upset about. Looking through a rolled-up paper has offered children relief from boredom through the decades. At least this quiet activity disturbs a limited number of persons, usually only the child's parents and those accidentally poked with the paper telescope. After all, focusing on anything for longer than a few minutes can be an achievement for some youngsters. Focusing on the pastor or choir may result in also listening to the message.

As adults, we might take a cue from this childhood activity and focus on our call to discipleship. In a sermon recorded in Matthew, Jesus tells us that the gate that leads to life is narrow. We might think this part of his sermon was directed to the outsiders and his Jewish opponents, but the sermon was most likely delivered to his followers and would-be followers. The message is also for us. Entering through a wide gate is easy. We could follow a crowd through a wide gate. We could even get sidetracked when we come out on the other side. Passing through a narrow gate requires staying focused. "Stay focused," Jesus seems to say. "Do not yield to all the distractions."

The choice between the road to salvation and the road to destruction must be made over and over. It is easy to fall by the wayside. We rationalize that we have many more temptations than those people gathered to hear Jesus centuries ago. Our world is full of messages that assail our senses. Most of us are never far from both auditory and visual communication. We are pulled in many directions. We are offered myriad opportunities for serving others. Numerous church and community task forces and committees need our attention. Sometimes we would like to forget our priorities and take advantage of opportunities for a bit of fame or glory. Each new day challenges us to focus on the best use of our time and resources. Every morning we make the choice between either serving Christ fully and faithfully or "just this once" taking the wide and easy path through a wide gate crowded with fellow travelers. How do we keep our focus? How do we keep our motives pure? How do we thread our way through the narrow gate?

None of us is perfect. We often slip blindly toward that wide gate. Some time-tested disciplines can help us to stay focused. Being part of a prayer or Bible study group often requires accountability to the group. Establishing a regular morning devotional time can bring focus to each day. Not every morning will be an intense spiritual experience. The Scripture for some days will seem too long and boring. Some days will seem too hectic for us to be bothered with devotions. But starting the day by intentionally putting on Christ, like putting on corrective eyeglasses each morning, will put the day in focus. Christ will guide us throughout the day.

When we gather for worship, we might even use imaginary paper telescopes to refocus our minds on the message. The results could surprise us.

Prayer: God of judgment and grace, we ask your forgiveness for the times we have failed to stay focused on your will. Thank you for the lessons children give us. Be with us as we travel the narrow path of discipleship with you. Amen.

Wearing Out the Window

Read Luke 15:11–32.

It all began when our children first shunned our parental escort service and ventured alone outside our home. We began "wearing out the window" as the expected time of their arrival passed. We would watch out our front window to see if they crossed the street safely. As they grew older, we watched for their bicycles to come rolling safely around our street corner. Later, we watched for his or her car to turn into the driveway. When circumstances prevented us from accompanying them, we watched out the window for their happy return from summer camps, athletic endeavors, and regional musical competitions. As curfews were extended, they told us, "You don't have to wait up for me." We looked out our bedroom window when we thought we heard the familiar sound of the car approaching our home. When storms were rolling into the area and our children were traveling home on threatened highway routes, we watched out the window as the skies darkened or the world turned white with snow. Now we keep watch at the window for their arrival with their own children for long-anticipated visits with us.

We have never had to reluctantly advance a son his inheritance so that he might embark on a future that we knew was full of reckless, foolhardy, and dangerous choices. We have never had to deal with the heartache of watching an estranged child leave with bitterness and misunderstanding clouding our farewells. Many other families have faced that sorrow. When I was a youngster, a neighboring farm family had a son leave home in anger. His parents kept a lamp lit each night in the window facing their lane, a sign of forgiveness that guided and welcomed him home.

I think those parents must have been familiar with the parable of the prodigal son. In this parable from the Gospel of Luke, the father saw the lost son approach from a distance. He must have been watching out his "window" for him. Did the younger son's parents keep watch out the window every day, longing and hoping for his return? At night, did they wonder about his welfare? Did his mother look out the window as she prepared meals? Did she dash to the window when she thought that she heard familiar footsteps? Did she turn in disappointment when it was someone else instead of her long lost son?

This parable has many dimensions. To me it is a powerful metaphor of how God watches and waits for us to come back to a loving relationship. Just as earthly parents patiently and faithfully watch for the return of their children, God watches and waits for you and me to come home. God waits for us as we judge others and fail to see our own faults. God waits for us as we ignore the hungry and the homeless. God waits for us as we wound those around us with words and swords. God waits for us as we waste our lives and the resources given us. God waits.

The great joy we feel when a child finally returns home after suffering and struggling and refusing reconciliation is infinitesimal compared to the joy our heavenly Parent feels when we turn and come home. There is great rejoicing when that yearning is fulfilled.

Prayer: Loving Parent, the depth of your patience, forgiveness, and love are beyond our understanding. As we welcome our children home, help us to keep watch for them regardless of the pain they may have caused us. Be with us as we wrap them in forgiveness and have a joyous celebration when they return. Amen.

Symbols

Read Matthew 5:11–16.

As a young 4-H member, our oldest daughter Jan developed a keen interest in home decorating. She displayed her handiwork throughout our home. Jan decorated the nursery for her baby brother. Her macramé incorporating pieces of coal from my one-room school is suspended from the hame of a harness from her grandfather's farm. Generations are knotted together in that piece of craftwork that still hangs on our family room wall.

Jan further expressed her creativity in the light shades she made for the hall by dipping string into glue, wrapping the string around a balloon, and allowing it to dry. The balloon was then popped and the globe of string wired for light. The lights were beautiful.

I was struck with the symbolism of the light shining through that tangled bit of stiff string. I thought of how Christ's light can shine through our tangled lives. We made smaller globes of string and used them in arrangements at Easter and Christmas.

Over the years, the hall has been redecorated and the light fixtures changed. We have kept the small globes of string with gold roping tucked inside. The symbolism has been especially meaningful in times of grief and disappointment. God is with us in our sorrows, tragedies, and even in the mistakes of our daily lives. No matter the circumstances, the light of Christ can shine through. God will not be held back.

We need symbols because as mortals we cannot find adequate words to express our deepest feelings and beliefs. Our language fails to describe God fully. Some Christians use symbols extensively, others sparingly or not at all. The Roman Catholic and the Orthodox churches have long traditions of using beautiful icons, statues, and paintings to remind parishioners of their faith. Colorful banners, wall hangings, and stained-glass windows can be seen in the sanctuaries of many Protestant churches. Some choose windows of plain glass to symbolize their outward mission to the world.

Symbols remind us of who we are and what we are about. When we walk into a sanctuary, symbols help us to identify the congregation and what they believe. The whole church building and the contents of the rooms also serve as symbols of faith and give clues as to the priorities and mission of the congregation. Is the sanctuary the main focal point? Is there a large kitchen? A food pantry? A nursery? Youth rooms? Quilting rooms? Classrooms? A large fellowship hall? What expressions and priorities of faith are symbolized in the building?

In our homes, our display shelves and decorative objects symbolize our interests. Would a stranger coming into your home or my home know we were Christians by just looking around? The contents of our cupboards, closets, bookshelves, and magazine racks serve as symbols of our faith. Most of all our daily lives—even our tangled lives—can show God's love. Love shines through the maze of our daily activities, the moments of solitude, and the offerings of forgiveness. Love shines through.

Prayer: Thank you, O God of light and love, for the many ways our lives can reflect your care for us. Help us as we strive to let your light shine through us even in difficult times. By your power and grace, enable us to brighten the dark hallways of others. Amen.

Masks

Read Matthew 7:1 and 23:1–5, 27–28.

"Mom, could I just dress up in Dad's old clothes and go as a tramp?" asked our son.

"Mom, is my clown costume done yet?" asked our daughter.

The reactions to Halloween costumes varied greatly among our children. After much discussion, each child wore a mask and pretended to be someone he or she was not. They shared the enjoyment of later bedtimes, the thrill of being out after dark for trick-or-treating, and the resulting sacks of candy.

My own rural childhood never included trick-or-treating. It did include a crepe paper dress with a tightly ruffled skirt made by my mother on her treadle sewing machine. I don't recall whether I was pretending to be a fairy princess or Cinderella, but I loved that dress.

It is fun to pretend, to act as though we are someone else for parties and trick-or-treating. Outside of these socially acceptable situations, pretending to be someone else is considered hypocrisy. Jesus warned the disciples not to be hypocrites.

Jesus used the scribes and Pharisees as examples of hypocrisy. The scribes and Pharisees were distinct but overlapping categories of people. Each had important roles in their society. Biblical scholars believe that the roles of the two groups may have changed over time but generally agree that scribes were a professional class who had training similar to lawyers in America today. They were conservative, and their words were taken seriously as coming from those with authority. The Pharisees were mostly laypersons without formal theological training. They defined, taught, and attempted to live what they understood as proper behavior. They were especially zealous about the laws of ritual purity, tithing, food, and correct observance of the Sabbath. They believed that the soul survives death and is then punished or rewarded according to the law. They often failed to live up to their own stated beliefs.

When I read these passages from Matthew as a child, I thought that the scribes and Pharisees were a really bad bunch. I was glad that I was most certainly not like them! But as a mature adult, I looked in the mirror and saw (could it be?) bits of a scribe or a Pharisee in myself.

The scribes and Pharisees were laypeople! Professionals, but not priests or pastors or ordained clergy as we might call them today. Laypeople trying in their own way to keep God's law. I had become a little smug about God's choosing laypersons to be prophets and even to be the parents of Jesus. I liked accounts of Jesus' choosing ordinary men and women to be his disciples. I had failed to realize that Jesus also used laypeople as bad examples! And more important,

Jesus saw behind the masks of the religious people and the "plain" people alike. He saw who they really were—not just fishermen or tax collectors or outcasts. Jesus saw them as worthy persons, capable of being his messengers and disciples. Or he saw them as hypocrites.

The Pharisees and scribes did not always practice what they taught. The religious hierarchy covered their hypocrisy with the masks of self-righteousness, ritual, and long robes. Christians today are sometimes guilty of that same hypocrisy. We might even say, "Do as I say, not as I do."

As adults, we might wear masks because of shame and fear of rejection. We might raise our standing in the community, at least temporarily, by wearing masks of deceit. That deception might result in sweet earthly rewards. But masks are for Halloween. Put away your mask and celebrate the life given you. God loves, forgives, and accepts us as we struggle to live Christian lives of integrity.

Look behind the masks of those all around us, those whom we judge by the masks they wear. See God behind the masks of not only those we love and esteem, but also those we hold at a distance and consider much lower than the angels. See God in the messengers of his love, and in his most unworthy children, recognize God's enabling and saving grace.

Prayer: O God, grant us the courage to be ourselves. Be with us as we strive to put away our masks and reveal your love. Help us to see your children behind their masks. Amen.

Emptying the Suitcase

Read 1 Timothy 4:14–16.

When our oldest child was packing for his first church camping experience, I helped as much as I could (and as much as he would allow). I drew on my own childhood experiences as a camper, my motherly wisdom, and the realities of his current wardrobe that would hopefully make it past summer. After he was soundly asleep, his father and I tucked some special little surprises in the suitcase.

Early the next morning, off we went—two parents, one suitcase, one sleeping bag, and one unusually silent boy. Camp would be fun, he assured us, but he did not know any other campers. We left him standing alone at the registration desk, a bleary-eyed boy bravely waving good-bye. We wondered how we could leave our child with total strangers.

At home we wondered each day how things were going, imagining all sorts of good things and some not so good things. "He is probably swimming right now," or "Must be time for a nature hike," we said to ourselves. We remembered our own religious growth in significant moments around the campfire and hoped that he could also experience spiritual growth. He did not have a jacket. What if it rained or the weather turned chilly? Finally, the day came to bring him home.

Emptying the Suitcase

When we got to camp, a swarm of tired campers with lumpy sleeping bags and socks sticking out of suitcase zippers waited for their parents. Our son was not among the group. We checked the snack bar and the trading post. No son. His cabin was empty.

At last, through the trees we saw two grinning, dusty campers rushing down the rocky hillside trail. One was our son. He introduced us to his new friend. The two explorers told of their new discoveries of lizards and rocks, of bushes and birds. He assured us everything was ready for the return trip home. The neatly closed suitcase, perfectly rolled sleeping bag, and grinning boy were loaded into the car. As we left, he waved good-bye to new friends and watched out the back window until the camp disappeared in the distance. Our son kept up a steady chatter about adventures on the trails and prayers at the fireside.

Camp laundry needs to be done promptly. Anticipating sand, rocks, wet swimsuit and towels and, I hoped, nothing alive, I carefully opened the suitcase. I was totally unprepared for what was in the suitcase.

His clean clothes were still in neat undisturbed stacks. His unopened surprise gifts were still under the clean jeans. Evidently, he had not changed clothes all week. All of that careful choosing of clothing and none of the clothes used! His wardrobe for camping, including the clothes that would have been more comfortable for the hotter days, was as clean as when he left for camp. The gifts chosen just for

31

him were unopened. We never received an explanation. As you can imagine, this has become a favorite family story.

Remembering our son's first camping experience, I wonder how much of the suitcase of my life is an undisturbed stack of possessions and gifts—a suitcase left untouched, not just for a week but for decades. Not just my grandmother's hand-crocheted tablecloth and bedspread, not just the unused silver pitcher, but also gifts of service and love, of talents and time, all gathering the dust of neglect.

What opportunities have remained boxed? Have I worn old habits into the future when new habits would have given strength for the task? How often have my soiled garments of jealousy, resentment, or anger offended others? Would the new shawl of love shelter me from loneliness? Have I missed some great gift in my desire to keep the items on top undisturbed? What have I kept in my suitcase that could have been a witness to Christ, to someone yearning for a sign? What garments of faith, what joys and sorrows, what talents, have I kept hidden?

Am I too busy, too frugal, too afraid, to empty my suitcase? On the long journey of life, a heavy suitcase is a burden. If I unpacked more of my suitcase, could I finish my journey with a small carry-on?

Prayer: Giver of life and all that is in it, thank you for the special gifts given to us. Forgive us when we become protective of those gifts and keep them hidden away like a miser's gold, to be counted only in secret. Give us the courage to be generous and know that we will always have enough to share in our lifetime. Be with us as we risk rejection of our gifts. Enable us to graciously accept and celebrate the gifts of others as they also risk emptying their suitcases. Amen.

Jesus Wept

Read John 11:1–38.

Screams and then the sound—a sound I had never heard before but recognized instantly. The dying breath was being forced from our daughter Joan by the weight of the mobile home that had rammed against us. She lay a few feet from me. I could not move. My body also was trapped. I could not touch her, could not help her. I saw her spirit leave her body.

I gave Joan to God, not because I owned her or because God needed me to do so. I did it because God was there with us. I pictured putting her hand in God's hand. I gave her because God, as her spiritual parent, was taking over from her earthly parents. I was literally a mother to the end.

Then I prayed that I might die instead of Joan. That did not happen. Waves of pain engulfed me, and I prayed to be unconscious. That did not happen. I prayed for a miracle, that she might live. That did not happen.

My mind became a mix of images. Joan's husband Steve and my husband Wayne trying to get help. My screams and ambulance sirens. Powerful jacks and airbags. Emergency personnel loading me into the ambulance. The ride to our local hospital. Members of our Sunday school class lining the hospital walls as I was wheeled to a waiting helicopter to be taken to a Denver hospital. The chaplain, who had been our pastor and Joan's close friend, meeting the helicopter. Clarity and confusion, desolation and then comfort were all jumbled together within me. The surgery, the pain, and the comfort of having my sisters with me when Wayne had to return home were intermingled with memories and grief.

That was only the beginning of the grieving. The process of accepting our daughter's death and releasing her to God has been a lengthy, uneven journey. Wayne and I, our sons Jeff and Jim, and our surviving daughter Jan traveled separate roads in our grief. Wayne went to Joan's funeral, which had been planned by her husband and her brothers. Jan left her graduate studies at Purdue to fly home with her husband and toddler daughter. I remained sedated in the Denver hospital awaiting surgery. Wayne coped alone with the details and daily reminders. The idea of closure is popular but, in our experience, misunderstood and overrated. The grief process is never completely over. We now know a dimension of life and love that we had never known before and never sought. Grief does not go away; it only holds the heart in softer gloves.

A beautiful September evening had turned to tragedy. Wayne's birthday celebration was cut short by the clock and the evening shadows. Our youngest son left to play in the marching band at his high school football game. We left to take advantage of the remaining evening light to help Joan and Steve set up their mobile home across town. They were returning to our town to begin life as adults with new jobs, new opportunities, and plans for building their new home. Then a sudden downburst of wind blew the mobile home from the jacks, moved it six feet, and set it down on Joan and me.

People have asked what Scripture I found most meaningful in the following weeks and months. With medications scrambling my mind and vision, I did not read seriously for months, could not concentrate. But, even at the site of the accident, these words were with me: *Emmanuel, God is with us,* and *Jesus wept.* Those Bible verses, taken out of context, spoke to me of God's love and sustained us through the months and years ahead. Those Scriptures were in fact the only ones that I could remember. The hundreds of verses memorized as a child, the passages studied as an adult were buried deep within my mind and temporarily inaccessible. Two verses—not much, only crumbs from my large loaf of reading, studying, and praying, but they were enough.

God's strengthening love did not come because I earned it with those few words pulled from a broken heart and dimmed consciousness. It did not come to me because I had been such a good Christian, had never doubted, or had led a perfect life. God's strengthening love came as a gift of grace in my time of need. In the hospital, helpless, completely dependent on others for my basic needs, I was filled with a blessed assurance. I floated for healing before God on a raft of prayers not my own, prayers from those we knew in our faith community and those who were strangers to us. During this great pain and loss, I never felt apart from God. I did not feel punished or disciplined by God. Nevertheless, there have been times before and since that awful evening when my faith is barely the size of a mustard seed. I just squeak by with the minimum size. The mystery of faith is in the tiny mustard seed, a glimpse of greater faith to come. And for God that is enough. Emmanuel.

The times of grief always turn into past times. Memories of past times bless and burn. Memories murmur love songs in our hearts, singing softly of laughter and life. Over and over the Bible tells us that after the darkness comes the light. The Holy Spirit is with us now and is behind and ahead of us in our lives. We are not left desolate. Our patient, deep suffering can be a witness to others. Our scars are evidence of physical and spiritual healing, of the universal pain and grief we all share.

Prayer: Patient and loving God, we thank you for your continued presence with us when our prayers are sighs too deep for words and our pain is too much for even loud cries to express fully. There is much we do not understand. When your friend Lazarus died, you wept with his sisters. Weep with us now, and soften our grief with your love. As your tears mix with our tears, your comforting presence enables us to live. Amen.

The Greatest of These Is Love

Read 1 Corinthians 13.

She lay quietly in the bed, her frail body dressed in the clothing we had designed and made for her. My sisters and I stood around her bed and talked of ordinary things—canning beans, the cost of jeans, the antics of our children, our plans for travel. We giggled at childhood memories and wiped our tears for the tragedy of the illness that had silenced her laugh. She did not seem to comprehend any of our attempts at conversation. We talked to Mother, listened quietly for any response. We gave her tender hugs. When we kissed her forehead and prepared to leave, she seemed to be trying to say something.

"What is it Mom? We can wait," we said.

Her voice came softly. "I know you, and I love you."

Our human frailties are no match for a mother's love for her children. Those were the last words I heard my mother say.

The Alzheimer's disease continued its cruel course. We added her lost memories to our own memories and kept them for her. We now give those memories to our children and grandchildren. She was in the care facility for ten years. The decision to place her there was difficult for each of us. It was obvious she needed twenty-four-hour care. Dad had cared for her beyond what we children considered possible or safe. Finally, the long days and nights became too much of a burden for even him. He traveled from their farm home to visit her each day until he too entered the nursing home. His heart wounded and tired, his strength gone, he died before she did. Her life was gradually reduced to basic bodily functions, her heart still beating its stubborn rhythm. What else remained? Very little brain activity, the doctors said. But no one really knows what tiny spark of Mother remained, or what tiny element of recognition her spirit refused to relinquish. The inability to physically respond does not mean the ability to feel and comprehend is lost, as evidenced by those persons who have been in a coma and awaken to tell of being trapped in their bodies. But, Mother was not in a coma.

When she died, her brain was donated for research. Alzheimer's disease was confirmed. The brain exhibited extensive plaque that had resulted in the loss of many functions. Her love for her children and grandchildren will live on through more knowledge of Alzheimer's gained through the research enabled by her and others. Perhaps one day this terrible disease can be prevented or at least effectively treated.

Scripture reminds us that the "greatest of these is love." Love is a gift presented without expectation of gratefulness from the recipient. Love is shown in the act of forgiveness. Love is being physically present with a loved one even when it is assumed that person cannot comprehend or speak. Love is making hard decisions about appropriate health care.

For love never fails. Our faith and hope, and Mother's faith, hope, and physical condition could not match love.

God hears our cries, our pleading, and even our anger at illness. Through it all, God's love is the greatest of all.

Prayer: Loving Parent God, thank you for your unfailing love even when we fail to understand or reply. Wrap our hurting hearts and wounded spirits in your love. Even when our lives seem hopeless, grant us the capacity to give and receive love. Amen.

Moving Up

Read Acts 2:17 and 1 John 2:12–14.

I had almost dialed the familiar number before I sadly turned away from the desk. Long after the deaths of our parents, I felt the urge to phone them with some bit of family news. The sharing now comes in prayer.

It seems strange to be the oldest generation in the family. We shifted joyfully into the role of grandparents but failed to correlate that role with other probable changes. We wonder how life passed so swiftly.

Regardless of our age when our parents die, whether we are young, middle-aged, or elderly, that event brings unexpected emotions along with those we anticipate. The role of eldest generation catches us by surprise even if we have been caregivers of our parents as they declined physically and mentally. No ceremony marks this move up in generations. We are not crowned. We do not receive tributes from younger generations. No formal ritual universally recognizes this passing of authority.

Yet, the implications of this new role loom large. Supposedly, we are wiser. We should have wisdom, increased understanding, resources for abundant sharing, and a firm unwavering faith. Sometimes we do possess all of those traits. Sometimes we do not. We may or may not occupy a position of love and respect in our families.

The questions still come in the darkness of night. In the midst of blessed assurance is the acute awareness of our frailties.

Our culture celebrates youth not age. Mass advertising is full of products to forestall the effects of aging and give the appearance of youthful bodies. Generations are studied carefully as to their voting, spending, eating, and living habits. Yet, in a time when people are physically and mentally vital at greater and greater ages, we seem perplexed as to what role each generation should play.

Our congregations look in vain to society for guidelines. When should the mantle of leadership be removed from aging but still strong shoulders? Which areas of church life call for youthful vitality and which for the perspective of long years in service? How are older members recognized in the church hierarchy in addition to being the source of funds? How can the visions of the young and the dreams of the old combine for vital discipleship? The questions seem endless.

Finding the right answers is extremely important for the survival of our churches. Older mentors might help guide young parents through the maze of childrearing. Multigenerational sharing groups could help bridge the gap. Grandparents might read stories or rock babies and toddlers in classrooms and nurseries. Young adults might serve as energetic role models and leaders. Each congregation must prayerfully discern and celebrate the role of each generation. Each generation holds those who are wise and those who have failed to mature intellectually and spiritually. Jesus did not seem to require that a person be a certain minimum or maximum age to become a follower. As far as I have found, neither did he talk about retirement.

Our congregations might contain four or even five generations. What a rich source of talents! What a great storehouse of knowledge and experience. People who have witnessed and grown through tremendous change in their lives and in the world are in the pews. A generation of believers eager to try new ideas sits beside them. How blessed we are. And God is with us in every struggle and every triumph.

Prayer: O Lord, thank you for the privilege of sharing the gospel with a world longing for reconciliation and peace. Grant us wisdom as we move into the status of the oldest living generation. Let us be models of love, encouragement, and acceptance. Help us as we struggle with how best to utilize the gifts of each age group. Give us strength as we continue to live and spread the gospel. Amen.

Blow the House Down

Read Matthew 7:24–27.

My brother-in-law Russell, my husband, and I walked around the house, crept into the crawlspace, and checked the mortar of the stone foundation. As the current owner of the family farm, I felt a keen responsibility to be a good steward of the property. The Native Americans, who had built the front four rooms, and my great-grandfather, who had added onto the house, had used local limestone for the foundation. We imagined the effort it must have taken to quarry the stone and set it carefully in place. Even after over a century, the house sat securely and squarely on those stones. Only minor repairs of the mortar were necessary.

When I was a child, I shuddered at the image of the big bad wolf that blew down the houses of the three little pigs. Only the house built of bricks was safe, and our own home was built of wood, which in my mind meant sticks. Mother calmed my fears by telling me that it was only a story, only words.

Now I think of that story and of our family home when I read the parable about one house built on rock and another built on sand. The image of the house unable to withstand the storms of life is vivid. We who live in windy country have seen structures blown down and can easily relate to windstorms. Those who live in other parts of the country may visualize the house built on sand being swept away by floodwaters. We know that even houses built on strong foundations might not withstand severe winds or floods; for those storms, we need basements or boats!

As an adult, I have gone beyond the mere words of the nursery tale to see a deeper meaning. Likewise, just reading the words of Scripture is not enough. The words might sift through our consciousness like sand, giving a pleasant sensation, slipping conveniently into the background, and leaving only the remains of a sandcastle. Sandcastles do not survive the storms of life. The house built on sand is blown down or washed away. It does not last a century and certainly not for eternity.

The parable from Matthew is not about houses built of straw or sticks or bricks, on stone or on sand, but rather about hearing the words of Jesus and acting on those words, about having faith and living that faith. It takes a strong faith to survive the storms of life. Illness and death, conflict and confusion batter every life. Challenges huff and puff at our faith in season after season. What foundation could stand those assaults?

I was born and raised in a house built through the sweat and tears of others. I was protected from wind and rain, heat and cold in that house. It withstood all the storms experienced in that corner of Kansas, in large measure because of the strong stone foundation built years ago. I did not quarry, set, or mortar any of those stones.

It would be so much easier to just move into an inherited house of faith built on a sturdy foundation of stones lugged through life by someone else. But to have a house of faith that will withstand the storms of my life, I must quarry my own foundation stones to add to those inherited stones. I am too weak to carry them alone. I need the help of God and my faith family, but I alone must mortar the stones into place with my own Christ encounter. Acting on the words of my Lord fatigues me. I falter and fall, suffer bumps and bruises. The foundation is never quite finished. To withstand the pushing and pounding of life's winds and waves, the stones require repointing with the mortar of prayer and faithful living.

Prayer: Dear God, thank you for being with us when we are tempted to find quick and easy answers in life and in faith. Help us as we select the stones for our foundations of faith. Lend your strength as we carry and set those stones. Make your presence known to us as we replace or repair the mortar cracked by our sins. Grant that our foundations will support our earthly homes and that we might be enabled to withstand the storms in our lives that come when we least expect them. Amen.

Part 2

Around the Table

Preaching on a hillside or standing by a fire on the beach or sharing a Passover meal, Jesus frequently used eating together to illustrate his message. Today we remember that whether we eat at a polished table or around a rug in a tent, the important thing is not where food is shared, but that food *is* shared.

The Banquet

Read Luke 14:7–11.

In the early years of my lay speaking ministry, I had been studying this passage from Luke about the banquets. As with most Scriptures, these stories have many different dimensions. I often dream about the Scripture I am studying or the message I am preparing. My dream about this passage had an unexpected, and unforgettable, personal slant.

In my dream, I was invited to a banquet. When I arrived, I found myself at the most beautiful mansion and grounds imaginable. Small groups of important world and religious leaders were mixed with ordinary-appearing people, talking together quietly as they gathered under beautiful trees and among flowering shrubs. Some formed conversation groups at the edge of the marble patio. It was a peaceful and beautiful gathering.

I felt highly honored to be included in the guest list. I could not imagine how I had been chosen. As I walked among the guests, a bell was rung calling everyone to the table. The table was very long with place settings of silver, crystal, fine china, and engraved place cards on white linen damask. Beautiful trays of colorful fruits formed the centerpieces. I wandered around the lower middle of the long table, thinking that would be the highest that I could hope to be seated (but forgetting to do as Scripture indicated and start at the foot of the table). Not finding my name, I did begin working my way downward. The places were filling, and I had not found my name. Those seated near the head of the table kept smiling at me. Could I really be seated there? Knowing others were more deserving, I continued to search for my name. The many titles on the place cards indicated persons of importance. Yet, in Christian discipleship, does a title matter? Most of the chairs were filled. Each time I glanced nervously in the direction of the head of the table, people smiled invitingly to me. Finally, one person actually beckoned me to come.

I walked with as much dignity as I could muster, trembling a bit as I made my way past all of those kindly, friendly people—friendly, but much more important than I could ever be.

The Head of the table motioned me to come closer. He spoke in a soft voice. His eyes were kind. I leaned down to hear his voice more clearly.

"May I have a glass of water, please?"

I lowered my eyes in embarrassment, and for the first time saw what I was wearing. Over my simple dress, I wore a clean white server's apron.

I was a servant at the Master's table.

May you also accept the invitation to be a servant at the Master's table.

Prayer: Loving Master, we hold such contradictory feelings. Many times, we feel unworthy to serve you. At other times, we hope for a place of honor at your table. Help us to remember that the choice is not ours to make. Thank you for the invitation to wear clean white aprons. Amen.

Carrying in the Chairs

Read Romans 12:9–13.

We scrubbed the oak and ash woods, tightened the rungs, and glued the seat. The chair is good for many more years of use. I had chosen the chair when my siblings and I divided our parents' household furnishings after their deaths. Whatever monetary value the chair may or may not have is overshadowed by the memories it holds. The chair had provided firm seating for various members of our large family around the kitchen table in our farmhouse. We had carried this chair into the kitchen from other rooms for every family meal. Because the kitchen was small, the drop leaves of the wooden table were lowered between meals and only two or three chairs were left at the table.

"Carrying in the chairs" was the phrase we always used to indicate the task of getting chairs and putting them in the proper places around the table. Mom would ask us to "carry in the chairs from the other room." We used the expression "the other room" frequently. It meant simply a room other than the one that you were in at the moment. We would gather the chairs: the telephone chair from under the wall telephone, two from by the dining room stove, three from the dining room table, and one or two from the living room. Our chairs did not match. One chair had no back. Other chairs had missing rungs. Most were lightweight and easy to carry. Sometimes carrying in the chairs was a shared task; sometimes one child did it. We all knew how the chairs should be arranged around the table. We carried in the chairs, with our parents and any guests getting the best chairs. Each member of the family had his or her same special place at the table at each meal.

We were asked to "come to the table" when the meal was ready. There was a place for each of us at the table. As the plain but plentiful food was passed, the older children helped to serve the younger children. We were nourished at the table.

Dad or Mom always "returned thanks," which is what we called saying table grace. The prayer was the same at each meal, an original one that Dad and Mom had composed early in their marriage.

Sometimes we had some conflict resolution at the table! We were given moral guidance, we were called to accountability, and we were frequently forgiven. We knew that we were loved.

I doubt that our parents realized that they were giving us a theological understanding of what it means to be a part of a faith community, yet those everyday mealtime rituals were just that. In every faith community, parish, or congregation, someone has to carry in the chairs to provide facilities and hospitality. Our tasks as adult Christians change just as our chores changed when we were children. The chairs we carry as adults may be heavy, requiring all the strength we can muster. The chairs we carry may need to come from a long distance. We are invited to come to the table from other rooms, which may be big or little, across the street or across the oceans. Each room is an opportunity for ministry. Friends and strangers, invited and uninvited guests will be seated in those chairs carried from other rooms. Our chairs are ready to seat everyone at the table of faith.

As we come into our churches with praise and thanksgiving, we share our love with others. We are faced with resolving conflicts in the Christian community much more daunting than settling disputes between young brothers and sisters. We embrace forgiveness that goes beyond a childish "I'm sorry."

I hold each memory of carrying in the chairs from other rooms and gathering for meals as a model for our corporate and individual Christian lives. Thank you, Mom and Dad.

Prayer: Holy Parent, thank you for examples of homemade faith. Help us to remember the intentional and unintentional lessons of our childhood even as we mature in faith and discipleship. Be with us as we offer our examples of faith to others. Amen.

Hospitality

Read Psalm 104 and Romans 12:9–13.

My husband stepped slowly and carefully on the plank as he crossed the "bridge" over an open sewer. He was one of several delegates from our church world conference who were visiting local mission projects in the slum area of Rio de Janeiro. The neighborhood consisted of homes made from scraps of lumber and cardboard scrounged from local dumpsites. A woman stood at the door of her home with a welcoming smile. Her front room was bright and sunlit. There was no roof. A bicycle and a broom leaned against a wall. The second room had a roof and contained a simple table, one bed, and two chairs. One bare electric bulb hung from the ceiling. A jar with artificial flowers stood in the middle of the table, and a simple cross hung on the wall. Dignity and grace clothed the woman as she shared her home with strangers.

Later that summer, back in our own home, I cleared the clutter from the guest room bed, filled the carafe on the bedside table with water, shined the mirror, plucked dead leaves from the philodendron, and opened the blinds. In the kitchen, the aroma of a plate of warm cookies filled the air. We feel honored when people choose to share our home, and we attempt to be good hosts.

Welcoming expected guests is a pleasure for most of

us. The unexpected knock on the door might be another story. The late morning arising, the big project midway to completion, the weekday accumulation of mail and "stuff" piled on dining room chairs, all stand exposed when the door is opened to the guest who happens to be in town. We make excuses and offer the chair with the most flattering view of our housekeeping. We share what is available from the kitchen, offer our friendship, and hope the conversation covers the clutter. Even in those circumstances, we enjoy being hosts.

When we welcome strangers into our home as the result of storms, when we give emergency care to children, we feel that we are obeying the Biblical commandment of hospitality. We feel that by hosting strangers and little children, we are in some way hosting Christ.

Yet, I wonder, who would be the better hostess for God, the gracious slum dweller in Rio or myself? Can we be equally gracious as hostesses for God?

Who is the host and who is the guest? We fill dual roles in our lives, the host to God and the guest of God. Perhaps being the guest of God is the more difficult role. Acknowledging dependency is a role we might not welcome when we seem to be programmed for independence.

We would rather run our own inn. Yet, God the Host gives us a spacious courtyard filled with beauty and offers a banquet table overflowing with water and food for the body and spirit. Our Host offers us hospitality regardless of our response, keeps the gate to the garden and the door to the mansion open, and says to us, "Enter into my courts with praise."

Prayer: Great God our Host, we thank you for the wonderful gift of our earthly home and for the people who share that home with us. Help us to always be gracious and generous hosts. Help us to remember daily that we are your guests and that this home is a gift to be cherished, shared, and kept as whole and beautiful as possible for those guests yet to come. Amen.

Daily Rations

Read Matthew 25:37–46 and Micah 6:8.

Sharing food with strangers, enjoying family meals, celebrating the return of a wayward child, eating with outcasts, and feeding the multitudes—all of these and more events concerning food are recorded in the Bible. Many parables include feasts and banquets. Most of us remember the most important meal of all, the Last Supper, with special communion services. Christians everywhere recognize the significance of eating together with family, friends, their faith communities, and sometimes symbolically with tables around the world. God's people have honored their Creator from the beginning with feasts.

The church picnic to honor our pastor was a true feast. Families filed past tables crowded with fried chicken and sliced ham, with hamburgers and hot dogs. Plate space was somehow found for some of the potato and pasta salads and fresh vegetables and fruits. Brownies, chocolate chip cookies, cherry pies, and cakes tempted the most determined dieters. Large coolers held cold water and lemonade. The food was enjoyed under the shade of trees while the ever-present Kansas breezes cooled the crowd and tossed napkins across the grass. Teenagers took advantage of the abundance and went back for second and third helpings. One dimpled little girl reached her tummy's limit and slipped her half-eaten hamburger to the neighborhood dog that had crashed the party. Everyone agreed that it was a special time of food, fun, and fellowship.

Yet, some of us at the picnic felt uneasy. The pictures and sounds of the world's hungry intrude on our consciousness at the most inconvenient moments. Did we hear faint moaning in the distance? Out of sight, but somehow not out of the mind, stood millions of gaunt men and women holding silent babies, as children with swollen bellies moved ghostlike around their stick-figure parents. In a few places, corrupt officials kept the harvested or donated food stores safe from the hungry hordes. In many places, there was no food to hoard regardless of money or power.

The questions are haunting. Who will take the table to the hungry? Who will brave the chaos? How long before a well is drilled that gives cold pure water? Some of those hollowed eyes have seen the abundance of others. How long will they be content to stand at the boundaries and stare? What would you do to feed your starving child?

What is just in terms of the world's food supply? Should we have a free will offering to help alleviate hunger at each potluck or picnic? Should we have events to raise awareness such as a dinner where each person is served two ounces of rice, the daily portion for many in the world? What does the Lord require of you, of me, of all of us who call ourselves Christians?

Prayer: O God of justice and love, thank you for your world of plenty so graciously given to us. Help us both to celebrate your world and to share your plenty with those who have the least. Your Son ate with disciples, friends, and even tax collectors, but he also fed the hungry crowds. We fail to follow his example of celebrating and sharing. We waste more food than many people have available to them. Give us the insight to know what to do with our bounty and the courage to take action. In Christ's name we pray. Amen.

Dishrags

Read Luke 12:13–21.

When I was a youngster doing dishes, doing dishes, and doing dishes again, Mama would often ask if I was using a clean dishrag. Now, we always said *dishrag*, never *dishcloth*, and usually it was a rag—an old shirt, a piece of flannel pajamas, or even an old undershirt. Dishrag was the appropriate term. We would not have wasted scarce money on a store-bought dishcloth.

Except sometimes, when there was a bridal shower, someone would lavish love and beauty and give a new dishcloth—perhaps disguised as a doll or a fancy bow, but actually a store-bought, paid-for-with-cash, new dishcloth. The moment of new beginnings seemed worth the extravagance.

At some point in my life, after college and after I was married and became a citified adult, I stopped saying dishrag and said dishcloth. And that was appropriate. I bought dishcloths now.

A new dishcloth always gives me a little lift. I save the new one for dishes and use the old dishrags for scrubbing burned pans, cleaning grills, and wiping wiener sticks. Dishcloths are saved for the not so dirty, not so messy, finer things in life.

I do not always replace my dishrags as often as I should.

Somewhere under the kitchen sink there is usually an old, dingy dishrag with a bit of a stale smell. The middle is mostly holes. It is so softened with use that the little bit of texture, the little bit of roughness that cleansed so well, is now worn smooth. There are even some strings hanging loose about to separate from the body. The extra threads and tighter weave of the border hold the rag together. I have used this dishrag to wipe away leftover crumbs, to wipe up the spilled honey that added sweetness and flavor to morning biscuits. This dishrag has been used to restore cleanliness to dishes and pans so that those dishes and pans are fit for future meals. It has been part of my equipment needed to serve. Now it is no longer serviceable and must be replaced.

My worn-out dishrag might be a metaphor for our lives as Christian servants. Our lives might look good around the edges and still work at least to some degree, but at the center things seem to be falling apart. We are still able to do a little work, a little cleansing of soup pots, but the dishwater of our discipleship is lukewarm. We are tired. We have been mocked for some of our efforts. We are frayed and afraid. It seems safer to keep up appearances, to just go through the motions. We want to hoard what energy and resources remain. Like the borders of that worn dishrag, the strong borders of the faith community can hold us together until we once again plunge into the steaming dishwater of salvation and service, of grace and gratitude. We can emerge like a new dishcloth.

Not only our lives, but also our church facilities—the carpets, tablecloths, pews, playground equipment, and table tennis racquets—and our church programs are all the "dishcloths" of our discipleship, each designed for use in ministry. If the church is active, the carpet will become stained, the tablecloth torn, the pews scuffed, and the play equipment worn out. Remember why the tools were purchased. Each sign of wear can be a witness of Christian servanthood. Old tools will need to be replaced.

Unused tools cannot fulfill the purpose for which they were made. Take that new dishcloth out of the drawer and use it. You can buy a new dishcloth. Use your life. Someday you will have a new life.

Prayer: O God, Provider of all our needs, thank you for the tools of our lives that enable us to serve you. Grant us the wisdom to know that tools are to be used. Grant us the wisdom to use our tools as you would have us use them. Enable us to take our new tools to messy places. And grant us the wisdom to replace our tools as needed. Amen.

A Piece of Cake

Read 2 Corinthians 8:1–15.

Joan counted the people present at the table: two grandparents, one sister, one brother, two parents, and herself. The birthday candles were carefully removed, and then Joan cut the three-layer cake as evenly as she could manage into seven large pieces. We accepted her generosity with smiles, realizing the significance.

The meaning of "a little child shall lead them" was revealed before our eyes. Generosity is a trait that we think we have practiced as adults. We try to instill it in our children by example, but this act humbled us. Joan liked cake very much; she had helped mix the cake, licked the frosting bowl, and guarded the finished cake against mishap before her birthday dinner. Yet, she shared her entire cake without hesitation, keeping only the last wobbly piece for herself.

We sometimes hear of children emptying their piggy banks for some cause they have seen on television or read about in their local paper. Children open their hearts and minds and banks to those in need. Were you the adult who inspired them?

In our world of instant communication, it is easy to become overwhelmed with the needs of the world and pull back into our shells of self-indulgence. Joan gave away all of her cake to those who were celebrating with her. How do we recapture that innocent generosity and yet remain good stewards of our abundance?

Given our large cake of comparative wealth, are we as generous? How many strokes of a calculator does it take to determine our percentage of giving? In fact, giving is not as simple as sharing a birthday cake. With multitudes of appeals for our funds and with most of the appeals coming from worthwhile organizations who are good stewards of the donations, determining who gets how big a piece of our cake can be difficult.

Which groups are worthy of your gift? Which exemplify your beliefs and priorities and keep the least proportion for administrative costs? In our own case, we believe that our church manages the money most efficiently both locally and throughout the world. One hundred percent of the money we give through our church for emergency relief, to alleviate hunger, and for other needs goes directly to what we designate since all of the administrative costs are born by general offerings. Your church probably has a similar program. The millions of outstretched hands haunt us. Our cake seems so small. We can only give according to our means. We must give according to our means. Determining who gets a piece of your cake in addition to your church offering takes investigation and prayerful discernment.

The Christians who practice Christ's teachings on generosity and reflect the generosity of little Joan are so few that we regard them as saints. How many pieces will your cake yield? How big is your piece of cake? What would the world be like if we each kept just one piece of cake for ourselves and gave the rest away?

Prayer: O Lord, Giver of all that we have, we admit that generosity does not come easily to most of us. The more we possess, the more we want. Keep our hearts from becoming numb to the needs of the world. Keep our minds open to discerning the best way to share our cakes of wealth. Amen.

A Taste of Weevils

Read 2 Corinthians 5:16–17.

I had the menu and the order of preparation for our Sunday lunch in mind: take some turkey slices and a jar of turkey broth from the freezer; thaw the slices and broth in the microwave while cooking noodles for a turkey, noodle, and dumpling main dish.

The partially opened package of noodles in the kitchen was not enough, so I got a new package out of the pantry. Unfortunately, the package showed evidence of weevils. This was an unopened package, and I could have returned it, but I had planned a noodle dish for lunch. Usually, I am quite flexible. That day I was not flexible. I opened the noodle package. Scooping out the "clean" appearing noodles, I put those noodles in the boiling water.

I kept in mind that in some cultures, weevils and grubs are considered good sources of protein, and sifting out weevils is a common task for folks in other countries. As I wiped little specks of stuff and floating weevils from the sides of the pan of the boiling noodles, I rationalized that if I lost my nerve about actually eating any remaining weevils, I could pick them out. I put the remainder of the package of noodles in the colander, shook it vigorously, and through those holes in the colander a sizable colony of weevils appeared in the sink.

Still not to be deterred from the planned menu, I cut the turkey into small pieces in preparation for adding it to the broth and noodles. I did abandon the idea of dumplings.

With the broth thawed, I dumped it into the cooked noodles. It was not turkey broth! It was brown rice with beef and vegetable soup. I had not labeled the jar but assumed it held the same contents as other jars on that freezer shelf.

The turkey pieces went back into the plastic bag. I dished up the noodles, extra protein, brown rice, beef, and vegetables. We sat down to eat.

Cooked weevils and brown rice look a lot alike. I lost my nerve, and we had a good laugh as I ate my peanut butter sandwich.

I am afraid that there have been times in my Christian life when I have been just as determined (stubborn?) to stay with my original plans as I was determined to stay with that original menu. Being flexible, being willing to change, is sometimes necessary in order to have an acceptable outcome. Enacting program ideas just because those programs worked in other churches, just because the idea is new, or just because the idea is old seldom accomplishes the desired results. Flexibility is required for programs to meet the needs of the people and situation, yet remain true to the teachings of Christ. When we assume that all resources are the same just because they come from the same "shelf" without examining the contents carefully, the results can be unacceptable.

Someday I may manage to eat weevils. Learning to eat strange foods may be the least dramatic change required in my future. Our lives do not remain the same year after year. Children are born; loved ones die. We grow older and not necessarily wiser. We might even find it difficult to put away some of our childish ways. New leaders change the course of history. New generations have different priorities and lifestyles. Life demands change. God must smile at the paradox of our restless natures and our resistance to variations in our routines.

Conversion means not only a change of heart, but also a change in lifestyle. Answering Christ's call to turn around and follow him is a much bigger challenge than changing a menu. What are the many (and I hope very small) areas of my life in need of changing that I have refused to acknowledge? I am more stubborn than I realized. I need God's help and forgiveness. The weevils in the noodles have reminded me of that.

Prayer: Creator God, give us the faith and strength for new opportunities and new challenges. Help us to honor the desires, strengths, and weaknesses of others. And remind us always to be flexible, to remember that there are many ways to nurture our souls as well as our bodies. Amen.

A Little Nail

Read Matthew 19:13–15.

My own place at the family kitchen table was on the long side in front of the south window. I sat between my older brother Sam and my younger brother Jim. Usually they were in place before me because I would be helping Mama fill the serving bowls. The more accessible spaces around our table were filled with the baby's highchair and other younger children needing help from Mom and Dad. To get to my place, I had to climb over two brothers' chairs, with or without the bodies of my brothers in place on those chairs, or crawl under the table and squirm up into position on my middle chair. A nail protruded from the underside of the table right under my plate. Sometimes I would scratch my head on the nail as I got on my chair. I was never scratched deeply enough to bleed. However, the nail was a challenge for me to meet at many meals at our table.

Why my parents, siblings, or I did not remove or bend the nail remains a mystery to all of us. Everyone knew it was there. The nail was not left because the rest of my family wished to taunt me, although I think that my brothers, being brothers, enjoyed seeing if I could manage to avoid getting scratched while crawling into my place. The nail was just an accepted fact.

You think that you would certainly have removed the nail. Maybe.

I wonder if there are "nails" that threaten our sisters and brothers in our faith communities, nails that we could so easily remove, but accept or do not even recognize as obstacles. Look for the nails: the only empty parking places far from the door, the one high step to the entrance, the heavy door, the low toilet without a handrail, or drinking fountains high on the wall. Can a talented vocalist who is physically challenged access the choir loft? The nails may be invisible but very real, such as the unwritten rules about how our game is played. Who is in charge of the kitchen? Are there economic or social restraints? We might even enjoy seeing others try to earn their places at our table.

How much time is wasted going around the nails? How many people do the nails wound? Does avoiding a nail increase individual worthiness? Or does being scratched by a nail give a sign of struggles overcome without help, a sort of badge of honor? Do I leave nails for myself to conquer so that I might indicate my superiority by overcoming them and show others how really worthy I am?

The nails that challenge those who might join us at Christ's table are many. Notice the nails. Welcome even the least of these—the little children, the crippled, the young mother with her hands full, the immigrant, the indigent, and your neighbor. Remove the nails.

Prayer: Dear God, we remember how you welcomed even the least of these, how you welcome even us. Be with us and help us to recognize and remove those little nails that hinder others from sharing sacred meals with us. Amen.

Chestnuts

Read Mark 11:25.

Have you ever eaten chestnuts? Roasted chestnuts? Here on the high plains, we do not have chestnut trees, and I have never met a family who roasted chestnuts over an open fire. But it sounds like fun. Recently, my husband and I decided to gather chestnuts at the supermarket. Neither one of us could remember tasting or preparing chestnuts. According to the package directions, the chestnuts can be roasted in a microwave oven for three to five minutes. Following those directions, I started my new culinary experience. While waiting for the chestnuts to finish their roasting, I went to the dining room to look at the mail. The sound of a struggling motor soon came from the kitchen. I hurried to the kitchen to find it filled with smoke. The cavity of the microwave was engulfed in flames. The chestnuts had been there for only two and a half minutes. Opening the microwave door shut off the fan inside and reduced the flames. I carefully carried the oven tray to the sink and scraped the flaming chestnuts into water. The chestnuts were burned to a crisp, and the house was permeated with a definite burned chestnut smell. I do not know whether the chestnuts were old and dried or the directions were incomplete.

After looking in cookbooks at alternative ways to cook

the chestnuts, I decided to boil the remaining chestnuts. After they had boiled for twenty minutes, we removed the shells and each of us ate a chestnut. The flavor faintly resembled that of peanut butter or, as Wayne described it, gauze. My cookbook had other suggestions for cooking chestnuts. I decided that enough was enough.

I am guessing that chestnuts are a survival food. If I were in a forest of chestnut trees, had an open fire, and the chestnuts did not burn up, they would taste pretty good, especially if I had wild blackberries to go with them.

I have other talents in the kitchen that are worthy. Someone else has the talent for chestnuts.

Not all of my attempts at Christian servanthood turn out very well either. I have not been burned literally, but I have felt the flames when I tried to practice servanthood in ways not suited to my talents. When I jump in with opinions just to get my own voice heard, I scorch the results.

I did not intentionally ruin the chestnuts. I do not intentionally wound others. Yet, those accidental wounds still cause pain. And just as the smoke and odor from burned chestnuts linger, so hurt feelings and misunderstandings linger. My apologies have not erased the words, only blurred them. Likewise, I have been unintentionally wounded. Some wounds leave scars. The scars are evidence of healing. Clearing the air of the smoke from our mistakes and our lingering negative attitudes requires maturity and humor.

Prayer: O God, we thank you for your forgiveness. Forgive us as we forgive others. Thank you for a sense of humor that sometimes is necessary for us to practice forgiveness. Help us to keep a sense of perspective as we suffer or inflict unintended wounds. Amen.

Teatime

Read Revelation 3:15–16.

For those of you who are not tea drinkers, this is Teabag 101. Tea is truly an international beverage, served in our homes, in tents in the desert, and in manors on grassy estates. Almost all tea now comes packaged in teabags, not only in the United States but also around the world. Paper envelopes protect the flavor, fragrance, and freshness of the tea and keep the teabags clean. On the paper envelope is the label indicating the maker, the type of blend, and the directions for use.

When I first saw the instructions "Lift here. Pull up gently." on a teabag of an English blend, I was struck with their meaning for us as Christians. We too can be lifted here and now by God—lifted at this place and at this time in our lives, not after we have changed our habits, lost weight, finished a degree, or finally have our lives together.

Here means literally in this place or at this point. Moses was lifted up in the here and now, before he was granted special gifts. He was lifted up for service in the here and now with the promise that God would be with him. Where you are, where I am, at this moment, God lifts us up in love.

In the parables, we learn that Jesus literally lifted up those who were ill, hungry, or thirsty. He even lifted up young children and refused to send them away. We can be lifting others here and now. Lift here!

I followed the directions on the teabag and lifted the tab. Under the tab, the words on the paper read "Pull up gently." God pulls us up gently from our failings, our fragile faith, and our fear of the unknown. Gently, yet firmly, we are pulled, and gently we pull up others. Church is not the place for you or me to be yanked around or to yank around others. Does someone need to be held accountable? Is someone in a pool of self-pity? Is someone afraid or lonely? Then pull up, firmly but gently.

We pull up gently on the teabag so that the little label at the end of the string stays attached to the bag. That label tells us the name of the tea and who made the tea. The teabag is clearly identified as to name and maker, both in and out of its protective envelope. As Christians, we are never separated from God our Maker, whether we are in a protective environment or out in the world.

We are ready to make a cup of tea. It is time for the hot water. The whole purpose of that teabag is to make tea, to make good tea. To do so, the teabag must be subjected to hot, boiling water—not a quick lukewarm dunk, but completely covered with freshly boiled water and left to steep awhile.

Lukewarm Christians do not make a difference. So each disciple, each follower of Christ, including you and me, will find himself or herself in hot water sooner or later. If we are Christians, even if we are Christians known by our love and gentleness, we will at some point find ourselves in hot water. At some point, we will be at odds with the world. Hot water will cover us—not a warm, soothing bath, but hot water that causes blisters and, perhaps, scars. We may or may not suffer physically or even be killed, although that is always a possibility. We may or may not have worldly success and then lose it all, but such dethronement is always a possibility. We may suffer from frustration and disillusionment and feel misunderstood. To be a disciple of Christ in mission is to expect to be in hot water.

For some, the hot water bath will be brief and for others extended. The longer the teabag is in the hot water, the stronger the tea. We might need to steep for some time to make our witness strong. If we read the Gospels carefully, the indication seems to be that if we are not at least occasionally in hot water as Christians, we might wonder if we are being authentic in our faith.

My teatime has become a time of reflection on my relationship with God. Lift here. Pull up gently. Cover with boiling water and steep until the full strength is released, resulting in tea that is strong, fragrant, and refreshing to those who are tired and thirsty. And all the while, the teabag is connected to its Maker.

Prayer: Dear Maker of us all, we thank you especially for the simple pleasures of life, such as a good, hot cup of tea. Thank you for daily reminders of the costs of discipleship. Refresh our spirits, give us the strength to endure the hot water, and keep us attached to you. Amen.

The Tongue, Hallelujah, and Help

Read James 3:1–12.

The summer heat, intensified by the stove heat required to prepare the noon meal for the haying men, filled the farmhouse kitchen as we quickly washed the dishes. My girlfriend was spending the afternoon at our house. We had been granted permission, for the first time, to make lemonade and cupcakes to take to the field for the men's afternoon break. We wanted this treat to be special. We chose a favorite cupcake recipe that we had made many times as eleven-year-old members of 4-H. We chattered and giggled as we mixed the batter, filled the pans, and slid them into the oven. The cupcakes baked to a fragrant and light perfection.

We gently wrapped the cupcakes in a fresh white tea towel and carefully placed them in a clean milk bucket to take to the field. A large jug of fresh lemonade completed our cargo. Anticipating the gratefulness of the men and their surprise at our baking expertise, we trudged through the pasture. In the shade of a big cottonwood tree at the edge of the field, the tired and thirsty men waited for us.

Just one bite of those lovely cupcakes started the men hastily reaching for the lemonade and gulping cups of the cool liquid to soothe their tongues and throats. They laughed and coughed, but did not congratulate us on our cooking skills.

In our Scripture, James cautioned that saltwater cannot yield fresh water. My friend and I had learned that a measuring cup mistakenly dipped into a canister of salt does not yield a cup of sugar. I learned that day to choose my words carefully. I had not specified to my friend which canister at the end of the cupboard contained the sugar and which the salt. My innocent mistake had ruined our cupcakes.

Why did James single out our tongues as so dangerous? The tongue tastes the good things of life—birthday cake, or a refreshing glass of lemonade on a hot day. Only if we have a sore tongue do we pay much attention to that part of our bodies. But James knew the importance of the tongue. The tongue gives us the ability to bless or curse, to lead in the right direction or cause to go astray, to build up or tear down.

Did our mothers remember this passage of Scripture when they cautioned us to "think before you speak" or "mind your tongue"? We are created in the image of God; if we are to glorify God, we can neither slander nor curse our neighbors. James stressed that we should choose our words carefully—whether we are giving directions, teaching, witnessing, or just engaging in ordinary conversation.

A casual exchange in the coffee shop might be an unintentional moment of divine encounter for someone at the table as well as for the speaker. Or a confidence might be overheard, repeated, and cause harm to others. Sometimes misunderstandings can be serious. The gospel message can be easily distorted by misuse of words. Those who lead others on their Christian journey need to be especially careful of what they say. Sometimes we touch the lives of people with our words when we least expect it. We teach even when we do not realize we are teaching. God uses our tongues in spite of ourselves. Hallelujah!

The writers of the letters in the New Testament used the means of communication available to them. They wrote, spoke, and lived the Gospel. They used their tongues for prayer and praise. Today, either in or out of church, the blessings and deceptions of our words are multiplied by the wonders of technology. Our tongues can speak across thousands of miles in seconds. Our words may be heard or read not only by the intended receivers but also by countless unknown individuals.

Our responsibility as Christians to speak carefully is even greater today than in years past. James told us to take that responsibility seriously. God inspires and directs us, but God is not a ventriloquist making certain that only acceptable, holy phrases come out of our mouths. We need to use our God-given wisdom and discernment when we use our tongues. We need God's help.

Prayer: Creator God, thank you for the wonderful gift of verbal communication. We know that sometimes we use our tongues to give curses instead of blessings. Forgive us when we speak before thinking, in anger or in jealousy. Let our words always be acceptable to you, O Lord. Amen.

Part 3

Games We Played

My brother Jerry spent several months teaching in Nigeria. He brought back the game called Adi or Mancala. It is an ancient game played with fields represented by shallow depressions in a board and grain represented by marbles, seeds, or stones. The depressions that tribes made to play this game centuries ago are still visible in the rock today. When my husband's parents traveled to Alaska and to Australia, they brought back games with the parts made of indigenous materials but played by the same rules. Many games have universal appeal, with variations of the same game played all over the world. Games can also be metaphors for elements of our faith. God is truly everywhere.

Ready or Not, Here I Come!

Read Acts 9:1–19.

In the early summer evening, our children joined their friends in a game of hide-and-seek. They celebrated their newly granted permission to stay outdoors in the gathering darkness by bravely going between dark bushes, crouching by dark porches, and hoping to be safely hidden before "it" called out, "Ready or not, here I come!"

That aspect of the game can be used as a metaphor for an important facet of our relationship with God. Sometimes God says to us, "Ready or not, here I come," or "Ready or not, come with me." He finds us in dark valleys, in our homes, and on the road. He comes in the night and in the day. God doesn't wait to come to us or to call us until we think we are ready.

We read in Scripture how God came to people when He was least expected. Like young Samuel, we might be afraid to tell others of our encounters with God because we feel we are too young or too inexperienced. When we were younger, like Abraham and Sarah, we may have thought that we were prepared for God and may have given up waiting for him. In our old age, we may identify with the elderly couple and laugh at the preposterous promises God gives us. Like Jonah, we rebel against the idea of offering redemption to people we feel deserve punishment. We might even leave the country in an effort to avoid God and the mission given to us.

Mary was a young girl who was not even married when God chose her to be the mother of Jesus. According to our standards, she was definitely not ready. Mary heard God and accepted her role.

We expect to finish our work before leaving one job to go to another. We want to have time to make the proper arrangements. Yet, ready or not, the fishermen left their nets and followed Jesus.

Some of us are prone to forget essentials when preparing for an important event and, like the unprepared bridesmaids, we miss the celebration. Others of us are great procrastinators. We count on another day to make ready. We say we will increase our giving to the poor after the next raise but then find Christ at our door in the form of a derelict.

God comes at unexpected times to people we would consider the most unlikely to be chosen, like Saul, a persecutor of Christians. We can relate to the fear of Ananias, who was not ready to minister to such an evil person as Saul.

Is it possible to be ready for God? Will there always be things left undone, improvements needed in our spiritual lives? Or do we live our lives as best we can and pray for God's grace?

Ready or not, here God comes!

Prayer: Thank you, Lord, for finding us even in our hiding places and for bringing us out of our own darkness into the light of your love. Thank you for coming to us whether we are ready or not. Amen.

King's X

Read John 1:1–5.

When, as an awkward first-grader playing hide-and-seek with my schoolmates, I stumbled and skinned my knee, I would hastily call out, "King's X!" That phrase gave me a respite from the danger of being caught by the child playing "it." With King's X, I was temporarily safe to tend to my emergency. The term could be used by anyone and was honored by everyone in the game.

King's X has been used for centuries by children in England and the United States. The exact origin of the term seems lost although there are some theories. The X might be an abbreviation for excuse. In our country, King's X is more commonly used west of the Mississippi, and usually when a child calls out the phrase, he also raises his hands with fingers crossed. East of the Mississippi, the most often used term may be King's cruse.

Adults have no equivalent phrase to call a truce. We know that life demands more than crossed fingers or calls of King's X. As adults, we play the real-life game of hide-and-seek, trying to hide from disappointment, change, illness, and death. The "its" in our lives leave us bruised and broken. We become fearful of even relatively harmless situations. We long for a respite from the trials that pursue us.

Then we come to the Scriptures. We come to the cross. We read the Gospel of John, and we understand. As Christians, we have something better than just the King's X of childhood games. The King's X becomes the symbol of our King's cross.

The its that chase us and catch us are conquered not by magic words spoken or by a truce signaled with crossed fingers. The its of our lives are vanquished by the assurance that God is with us and with God we will have final victory. With the King's cross, life is an exhilarating race to victory over the grave. With our King, all the darkness that life might bring is overcome. The cross is the true King's X for our lives. Claim the cross.

Prayer: O Lord, sometimes we would like to be as children again, playing simple childhood games where we could just say, "King's X!" and have a moment of rest. Open our minds and hearts to the presence of Christ that we might have strength and courage when we feel chased by the misfortunes of life. Lead us to quiet places of rest. In Christ's name we pray. Amen.

Olley, Olley, Outs in Free!

Read John 3:16.

When we played our childhood game of hide-and-seek, the person who was "it" could call out, "Olley, olley, outs in free!" (You may have said slightly different words.) At that call, we could come out of our hiding places and not be considered caught. We were home free. Even if we walked slowly, we would not be caught. We could really come home free.

I remembered that game when I recently encountered John 3:16 again and read it with fresh understanding. The promise sounds almost too easy and yet too hard. It is easy to read and even to say, but to believe? Come home *free*?

African-American slaves understood this offer of freedom found in Scripture very well. The white masters allowed slaves to participate in Christian worship only at their discretion. Slaves were not allowed to have their own worship, and those few who could read had only limited access to Bibles. The slaves understood the night visit of Nicodemus as proof that it is possible to come to Jesus even when those in power forbid it. They held secret religious gatherings in their cabins at night. They were willing to risk their safety and their lives to come to Jesus, who offered true freedom. This freedom in Christ gave many of them the courage to seek physical freedom by the Underground Railroad.

John 3:16 gives this great promise: Olley, olley, outs in free! We are not slaves. We can read our Bibles without fear. In our land, we can worship where and when we please without the threat of beatings. If we believe in Christ, we are home free. No racing to beat it to the base. No special tricks required. Discipleship will have its own requirements of hard decisions and sacrifices, but grace is free. Just believe and accept the grace offered.

"Olley, olley, outs in free!"

Prayer: Triumphant God, as we sing praises for victory over death, grant us the courage to come out of hiding and hear once again, as when we were children, "Olley, olley, outs in free!" Let us begin, again or for the first time, our journey with you. Amen.

Stop the Merry-Go-Round

Read Exodus 20:8–11 and Matthew 11:28.

The merry-go-round carried its squealing passengers on wooden bench seats as it twirled faster and faster, propelled by the oldest and strongest students from our one-room country school. Although the merry-go-round provided a favorite form of play, its riders were not entirely safe from mischievous acts. The smallest children were protected and favored by all other students. Children in the middle grades and girls in seventh and eighth grades were considered fair game for pranks by the older boys. In spite of squeals and cries of "Stop the merry-go-round! I want off!" from passengers, those who powered the merry-go-round sometimes pushed even harder and faster. Jumping off was too dangerous. The only option was to hang on tightly until the pushing crew grew tired, the five-minute bell rang, or the teacher came to the rescue.

But those who pushed the merry-go-round were also at risk. As the speed increased, it became harder and harder to keep up and to control the speed. There was the risk of slipping and falling beneath the twirling bars. If the pushers were quick enough, they could hop onto the frame and ride in a crunched position until the merry-go-round coasted to a stop and everyone could rest.

Pushing that out-of-control merry-go-round. Even

rides we voluntarily choose sometimes overwhelm us. It seems that each of us has too much to do and not enough time—never enough time. We feel that we have no control over the speed of our lives. We are burdened with our own schedules, the schedules of others in our families, physical and emotional needs, the demands of employment, of business, of loan payments, of the expectations of others, and on and on. Adding the time necessary for spiritual growth, for worship, and for serious Bible study seems impossible. Sundays become a time to catch up on chores or even to work.

If we find time for a vacation or a long weekend, we are apt to travel as far as possible, fill the hours with activity, and return to our routine lives exhausted. Worse still, we seem to be teaching our children to live their lives at the same frantic pace. We take them to their ball tournaments, track meets, special lessons, and to activity after activity. We permit those activities to crowd out any observance of the Sabbath. We are the pushers of their merry-go-rounds, and our children cannot get off.

We assume that in ages past, life went at a slower, more controlled pace. Maybe yes and maybe no. The commandment that is recorded in Exodus, to observe the Sabbath and its required rest, indicates that even then people found it difficult to rest and faced many of the same burdens that we do. Scripture tells us to not forget the Sabbath and to remember to keep it holy. Early Christians chose to observe the Sabbath on the first day of the week to remember Christ's resurrection. We continue that today.

Jesus observed the Sabbath. He attended synagogue on the Sabbath as was his custom. The question is not *whether* the Sabbath should be observed but *how* it should be observed. Jesus demonstrated that too many rules defeat the meaning of Sabbath. Do what is holy, rest, and remember God. That seems straightforward; yet, for centuries Christians have struggled with what it means to keep the Sabbath.

Sabbath gives us permission to rest. That permission is given to both the pushers and the passengers on life's merry-go-round. Permission is given to stop the merry-go-round. We not only have God's permission to rest, we have God's command to stop and rest. The word *Sabbath* means "cease."

The children chose to ride the merry-go-round on that playground long ago. Today we choose to get on our own merry-go-rounds. We choose the speed at which we push our passengers. To keep the Sabbath means to stop the merry-go-round for at least one day.

> Observe the Sabbath:
> Rest.
> Remember.
> Keep it holy.

Prayer: Holy God, thank you for guidance and for the promise of your Son to help carry our burdens. Forgive us for over-scheduling our days, for forgetting that even you rested. We ask your blessing as we make those decisions that will allow us to rest, to remember, and to keep the Sabbath holy. Amen.

Knock, Knock

Read Mark 6:1–5.

Most families go through a period of knock-knock jokes. The span between the time when such jokes are considered very, very funny and the time when siblings roll their eyes if they hear one coming is relatively short.

These knock-knock jokes came from a grade school Sunday school class:

> Knock, knock.
> *Who's there?*
> Luke.
> *Luke who?*
> Luke who's there before you open the door.

> Knock, knock.
> *Who's there?*
> Esau.
> *Esau who?*
> Esau him looking out the window.

If knock-knock jokes were going around in Nazareth during the first century, perhaps one went like this:

Knock, Knock

Knock, knock.
Who's there?
Jesus.
Jesus who?
Jesus the Son of God!

How would the people of Nazareth have received such an answer? How would you have answered that question?

Nazareth was a small peasant village of about 1,200 to 2,000 people. Jesus spent much of his short adult life there engaged in woodworking. We assume nothing was unusual about his trade. After Jesus left Nazareth to teach and preach around the country, he came back to his hometown. He was a different person. He was making outrageous claims. The people of Nazareth might have been a little jealous. It is easy to imagine the locals saying, "Where did Jesus get all this knowledge, this wisdom? We know how long he was in synagogue school. Let's take him down a notch or two. Keep him in his place!"

In their minds, they had cause to be offended. Jesus was an embarrassment to them. After all, why wasn't he at home helping to take care of his mother and the rest of his family instead of off preaching like a know-it-all?

Jesus had preached successfully in other villages. The people in his hometown of Nazareth did not seem capable of knowing Jesus as the Son of God. That God had become human and lived in Nazareth was mind-boggling to the

Nazarenes. It is mind-boggling to us even now. Like the Nazarenes, we find that the incredible gift of the Incarnation is hard for us to open.

Jesus who? Each of us must answer as an individual. Our answers might change over the years. An answer might come either in a single dramatic moment or slowly and quietly. No matter how long we might live, it will not be long enough to fully answer the question, to know the fullness of God in Christ. Like peeling an onion, we peel back layer after layer of meaning to Scriptures as we study and pray, as we grow more mature in our faith. When we peel this onion of increased understanding, we cry, sometimes with awe, sometimes with praise, sometimes with guilt, and sometimes with the joy of being forgiven, as we recognize Jesus in more and more ways.

> Knock, knock.
> *Who's there?*
> Jesus.
> *Jesus who?*
> Jesus the Son of God!

Prayer: O One God, forgive us for not recognizing you in our daily encounters. Open our eyes, ears, and minds, as we go deeper and deeper into our relationship with you. Help us to recognize you. Let us not be afraid of knowing who is there. Amen.

What's Your Trade?

Read James 1:22–25.

The basement in our one-room school was a source of pride to us. The coal furnace sent warmth to the floor register by the teacher's desk upstairs. To the right of the furnace, an old wooden kitchen cabinet held a few pots and pans in readiness for community dinners. The long wooden table by the north wall held current student projects, potluck dishes, or games, depending on the season. At the other end, at the base of the stairs, shelves and tables held a large clay jar of drinking water, tin cups, and a hot plate. A tall slender "shotgun" cream can filled with water stood next to an enameled basin for washing hands. North of this area was a coal room and a storeroom.

The most wonderful part of the basement was the large open space in the middle where we played games on days when cold, rain, or snow kept even farm children inside at recess. Games of drop-the-handkerchief and tag smudged the hopscotch diagram drawn in chalk on the cement floor. A favorite game included pupils from all eight grades. We called this game "New Orleans." It was a charade type of game. In our version one team questioned and the other team answered.

Team 1: Here we come.

Team 2: Where you from?

Team 1: New Orleans.

Team 2: What's your trade?

Team 1: Lemonade.

Team 2: Show us some if you're not afraid.

Then the first team acted out the trade for the second team to guess. The team's trade was identified by the actions of the players, not by verbal clues. You may remember your own versions of charades, played as children and now as adults at fun evenings with family and friends.

Imagine that you are playing this game as a Christian. Where are you from? Who are your folks? People enjoy knowing about their ancestors, learning where and how they lived. As people of God, we have roots going back to Old Testament times. We are adopted children of Abraham. As Christians, we include all those saints before us and around us on our family tree.

Where are you from? Do you live in a basement? In a high-rise apartment? In the city or in a rural area? What tools for living are in your home? How do you use those tools?

What's your trade? What is your "recipe" for your lemonade? Is it a secret recipe that you do not share? Is it your own recipe, or does it belong to someone else? What taste does it leave on the tongue, sweet or sour? Does your trade reflect your Christian faith?

How do you act out your faith on a twenty-four-hour basis? Does your daily living lead others to identify you as one of God's children?

Our Scripture reading is only one passage in the Bible that can help us make our own recipes for lemonade. You may choose other passages. Your recipe for lemonade and your trade will be different from mine. Each of us is a unique child of God.

Write down your recipe for living a Christian life using the ingredients that you are given. Act it out. Live it daily. The other team is waiting.

> What's your trade?
> Show us some—
> And don't be afraid.

Prayer: Creator God, who molds and makes us brothers and sisters, each unique and precious, help us to choose our trades wisely and to serve with courage, quietly and humbly. Amen.

Part 4

Common Threads

When we had exchange students in our home and when we visited other lands, our understanding of other cultures was greatly enriched. Over and over, we could see that certain things are common to each of us no matter our geographic address. All parents worry when their children leave home. All parents want the best for their children. All over the world, families face the challenge of change. New ideas, new inventions, changing cultural standards— each challenge must be met. Living means changes in our bodies and in our status in our communities and families. These common threads weave together people around the globe in a wonderful multicolored tapestry.

You Can't Snap a Hook

Read 1 Corinthians 12:4–26.

When teams were chosen for the schoolyard game of softball, I remained on the steps as usual. Cross-eyed and uncoordinated, I was not good team material. Although I once dreamed of pole-vaulting with my cane, I am no more athletic now than I was as a child. I am simply not interested in football, racing, or the many other sports that are often used as sermon illustrations. However, since my preschool years, I have been fascinated by clothing design and construction. I have attached many garment closures, including countless snaps and hooks.

One morning as I was trying to fasten a skirt with my mind in a sleepy fog, I realized that I was trying to snap a hook. It would not work. When I make a skirt, sometimes I may sew on a hook, sometimes a snap, or sometimes both, as men's trousers may have both a hook and a button. As I tried to snap that hook sewn next to the snap, even in my sleepy state, it became obvious that you cannot snap a hook or hook a snap. Snaps and hooks both perform the same basic holding-together function, but they perform that function differently.

That morning when I tried to snap a hook, I was reminded of the common purpose, beliefs, and heritage we share as Christians and yet how different we are in the details of our interests, gifts, and talents. Snaps and hooks, though they are different, share the purpose of holding a garment together. To fulfill that purpose, they must be attached to the garment. Christians share the common purpose of serving God. To fulfill their purpose, they must be attached to the garment of Christ that is the church.

Christians serve in different roles in their congregations. Jesus chose very different persons to be his disciples, from Mary and Martha to Peter and the rest of the twelve apostles. Paul made disciples in prison and in scholarly circles, in homes and in the marketplace. In spite of these examples of diversity and our own common sense, we act as though other Christians should all be like us or at least mostly like us. We keep trying to snap hooks or hook snaps.

Like snaps and hooks, we need to be attached to the garment of Christ's church. Enabling each other to function at the highest level will hold our communities of faith together. As snaps, we may hold firm to keep priorities in place. As hooks, we may pull together differing viewpoints. Sometimes a hook is best. And sometimes a snap is best. I need both in my sewing cabinet. The church needs both in its membership.

But, remember, you can't snap a hook.

Prayer: O God, Thank you for the great variety of people and gifts in your church. Help us to accept our own unique gifts and the unique gifts of others, that your church might be complete. Amen.

Full Price

Read Micah 6:8.

Another sales catalog slips from our stuffed mailbox. Merchandisers know that some of us have a love of shopping. Particularly *bargain* shopping. If we want to experience a real high, we head for the fifty-percent-off page or rack. We rationalize our buying by convincing ourselves that at bargain prices we must buy even if the items are not on our shopping lists. This habit is encouraged by weekly bargains, sales catalogs, and radio and television commercials. Buying a needed item at a sale price is sometimes a wise action. It can help stretch the small church budget or enable a family to purchase school clothing for their children. Buying needed items at end-of-season clearance prices can allow the purchase of higher quality and longer lasting items. And it helps merchants reduce their inventory.

Shopping can be either good or bad. As Christians, we realize that every dollar we spend reflects our Christian values. In our church, we have studied consumption patterns, the terrible conditions of some third world workers, and the exploitation of children in the workplace. The abuse of workers in order to keep unit costs low and profits high is well documented. Yet we relish the ability to have more possessions at less and less cost to us. When our closets and garages become too full of stuff, we have a rummage sale, then send boxes of leftover used clothing to missions, and feel very good.

We need to consider many questions before we go bargain shopping. Who helped pay the real price of this item? Was it an underpaid worker, a child laborer, or a small merchant no longer able to make enough profit to support his family? Was it someone in a developing country who can no longer sell locally made goods because of the flood of used clothing? What natural resources are wasted as a result of our overconsumption?

Most important, has the desire to always get the best bargain seeped into our spiritual lives? Have we assumed that easy living is our much-deserved reward? Do we search for the least demanding spiritual discipline, the least costly tier of giving? Do we demand the preaching that least disturbs our status quo?

What does the Lord require? Full price! God does not offer a bargain basement, commitments for sale at fifty percent off. The Lord asks that we pay the full price of discipleship. God sets the same price for each of us. Micah tells us the requirements. We are to do justice, love kindness, and walk humbly with God. We respond according to our talents, our resources, our place in life, and especially our willingness to say, "Here I am."

We are not asked to wait to respond until we have what we consider an adequate bank account or status or the price is reduced. When we have prayerfully determined the full cost and attempted to pay that price, we still feel inadequate because nothing we can pay is equal to the price paid once and for all for each of us. Because Christ has paid the full price for us, our chance to say "Here I am, Lord!" is too good a bargain to pass up.

Prayer: O Lord, what do you require of us? We give some of our possessions. We give some of our time. We hold on to too much. Micah makes your requirement seem too simple—and much too hard. We do try to practice justice, to love kindness, and to walk humbly, but be grace-full, please, O Lord, in accepting our offerings. Amen.

A Seamstress

Read Acts 9:36–43.

Dorcas was dead, and the widows wept. Who would make their clothing now? How could they survive without the generosity of Dorcas? Widows, who had very few opportunities to earn money to support themselves, were some of the most vulnerable people of their society. Dorcas, also called Tabitha, known for her good works and her charity, was the only woman in the Bible to be called a *disciple*.

The widows were ready for a miracle in their distress. Peter, remembering the power given to him by Jesus, asked the congregation to leave. He prayed and then went to Dorcas and raised her from the dead.

I can identify with Dorcas in this story from Acts. Dorcas was a seamstress. My sisters Shirley and Carol and I are seamstresses. Several years ago, we put our skills to a special purpose. Hundreds of colorful dresses hung on the racks in the many stores where we shopped for our mother, who had recently moved into a long-term care facility. We pushed hangers, read laundry instructions, and noted the designs. None of the dresses were appropriate for our mother's special needs. Using our skills from years spent sewing clothing, my two sisters and I designed patterns and made Mother a suitable, stylish wardrobe.

As a result of that experience, we embarked on a fifteen-year business adventure making clothing for people with special needs. Toddlers, young professionals, people living at home, and people living in care facilities all appreciated having fashionable and functional clothing. Persons for whom dressing each morning had been a painful ordeal could now dress with comparative ease. Their wardrobes no longer labeled them as dowdy and disabled. When circumstances forced us to cease our business, I felt a void in my life. Making those garments had been a means of living out our faith. It was one of our ways of being disciples.

Sewing and other simple everyday skills can be used to serve others. Many people use their skills to make wardrobes for missionaries, clothing for tiny premature babies, warm sleeping bags for the homeless, blankets for children in shelters, or caps for those undergoing chemo for cancer. Someone is always waiting for that touch of love expressed in a simple form of help. Strong arms can carry in groceries. Neighbors can bring in the mail, shovel snow, or cut grass. The family cook can make an extra casserole. The list of needs and simple skills to meet those needs is endless.

Dorcas demonstrated God's love by using her talent to make clothes for the least of those in her society, the widows. Peter dramatically demonstrated God's generous love when he raised the disciple Dorcas from the dead.

A Seamstress

Prayer: Loving God, we thank you for our abilities to do those everyday tasks that make our lives enjoyable. Help us to recognize the potential for service using our everyday talents and abilities, which we have considered ordinary and unimportant. Open our eyes to see those who need just what we have to share. Amen.

Elvira's Dress

Read Ephesians 4:22–24.

A picture in my old family Bible dates from the mid-1800s. The picture is of a mother named Elvira and her three daughters. They presented a somber appearance; each woman wore a finely made black taffeta dress.

My grandmother told me about those dresses. It was common, she said, for women of the frontier to have one nice dress. The dress was usually black, but might be made in a fine white lawn, a prized cotton fabric. The dress was made when the young woman was married or for another special occasion. Elvira wore her dress for funerals and weddings until it no longer fit the stooped shoulders and the back broadened by wood gathering, harvesting, and washing clothes.

As the years passed, the dress was carefully kept in a trunk. When illness came and Elvira's body wasted away, the dress once again fit her slender body. The dress became a mantle of the memory of that vibrant young woman of the past and a tribute to the courage and beauty of Elvira.

Sometimes I think that our churchwomen's organizations are like that pioneer woman's dress. Our organizational pattern has served us well. The fabric that clothes our women's groups is made of the warp and woof of prayer and study groups before us. The selvedge of missionary societies provides a firm frame for our activities.

This dress of my group has some red stains from communion grape juice and wedding punch, some oily spots from chicken salad served at funeral dinners, and a bit of blood from fingers pricked at the quilting frame. There is a worn spot from children who leaned against the knee at after school programs, and a faint stain on the shoulder from a baby rocked to sleep in the nursery. The shoulders are padded, and that is a good thing; there were times when we wished for larger shoulder pads during some rough patches of unpopular decisions and statements. The hem has been taken up and let down several times, the buttons moved hither and yon, some elastic added in the waistline as needed for pregnancies, all in an effort to fit the next woman who put on our church dress.

But, frankly, the dress is looking a little dated. It is, after all, a grandmother's dress. The basic style is a classic. Changing the trim and buttons might help, as would doing the hem again. Maybe it could even be patched where it was torn on the last mission trip. Surely the dress can still fit the spiritual needs of a new generation of women. But maybe not.

In the clothing industry, basic patterns called slopers are made in different sizes and are the basis from which current styles are made. Ease is added for wearing and style, allowing two dresses made from the same sloper to be very different in appearance and yet fit the same size body. Should our church organization dress, which has identified us and served us well, be taken apart and used as a sloper to provide a basic tried and true foundation for a new dress?

Many women, even in our own congregations, shiver in spiritual winters because they lack the warm clothing of faith that we ourselves have found. Women everywhere are searching the clothing racks for a spiritual garment that will enable and protect them on their own spiritual journeys. The trendy faith dresses from bargain racks stain and tear when grief spills against the fiber. Faith dresses purchased at the current favorite boutique shop rip apart after a season of stress.

Somewhere, a new fabric is waiting for the new pattern—a bolt of fabric even more sturdy and beautiful than the fabric we have loved. This new fabric has the richness of our heritage and purpose threaded in its warp and woof. Flecks of an entirely new fiber add texture to the surface. The fabric can be fashioned into a style with many variations and accessories.

Some of us will find the new dress difficult to recognize as a garment of faith. The style sketched by the younger generation has more wearing ease than the old style. Perfecting the pattern will require numerous fittings. It might mean some painful pricks of pins as young and old models squirm in protest. It might mean several dresses will be out on trial before the final garment is chosen. It will take willingness on the part of old and young alike to accept slightly different variations of that faith dress. Commitment and prayer, courage and persistence will be needed in large doses.

We really have no choice. We do not want our organization's faith dresses to become burial dresses. With God's help, we can fashion a new, appropriate style based on spiritual growth, scriptural knowledge, servanthood, and courage.

Prayer: Dear Lord of us all, weave us together with the bonds of Christian love. Give us strong threads that our new garments might hold us true to our faith as we change and grow. Help us to listen to you and to one another, to recognize the strength of youth and the wisdom of age. Hear our plea that we might continue in your service in ways unique to our time in history. Amen.

The Wardrobe

Read Matthew 25:31–40.

It is the end of the season. My stuffed closet must be sorted. I try to be realistic in deciding which garments go to the storage closet, which to missions, and which still have enough elastic for another season. I may keep a few things for their sentimental value.

Beyond the practical warmth they provide, the clothes we wear can bring back memories. When I was a child, some of my clothes were hand-me-downs from my cousin Marcia. When I wore those clothes, I thought of Marcia and she became a part of my day even though she was hundreds of miles away. When I wore the plaid jumper my daughter Jan made for me, I felt wrapped in Jan's love.

Clothes can make a big difference in our lives. The clothing we wear gives others their first impression of us. The impression may be incorrect, but clothes do project images of high or low status, of wealth or poverty, of laborer or professional. The deaths of two world-renowned women in September 1997 made me realize that when we decide what we will wear, we choose not only the image we want to project to the world but also how we will lead our lives.

I had admired the beautiful clothes, the public poise of Princess Diana. She did not wear a tiara in her everyday life, but she always looked the part of a princess. She was perfectly groomed even when she held a sick child, walked with her sons, or embraced a victim of a land mine. She was loved by the people and often used her position for good causes. Her funeral was attended by hundreds of distinguished and well-dressed world leaders.

Shortly after the funeral of Princess Diana, another service was held for a tiny, plain, wrinkled woman with a big nose, stooped shoulders, and bony fingers. She always wore the simple sari of white cotton trimmed in blue worn by all sisters of her order, which reminded me of the dishtowels we used for costumes in Christmas plays. Her name was Mother Teresa. She lived among and cared for the extremely poor on the streets of India. At her funeral Mass, the presiding cardinals were clad in elegantly embroidered robes and swung golden censers. About half of those at her service came from the slums of Calcutta. A leper, a woman released from prison, and a handicapped man carried in the elements of the Eucharist. Mother Teresa may be regarded as a saint.

That same weekend I watched a beauty pageant on television. Women in swimsuits and beautiful gowns paraded and pranced before the judges. Each woman also expressed her goal to do good for others during her yearlong reign. Each hoped to be declared queen of the pageant.

Those mixed images of wardrobes seemed to me like

a snapshot of our world. We tend to judge individuals by their clothing. How accurately does a wardrobe measure the Christian servanthood of the individual? Did Princess Diana use her position to the best of her ability to help others? Was Mother Teresa more holy than Princess Diana? And what about the young women in the beauty pageant? Were some of them planning to devote their lives to good works? What is excess and what is necessary to have in our wardrobes and in our lives?

What do our clothes say about us? How important are the clothes we wear in our Christian witness? Do our clothes help or hinder us in our mission to serve others? What about my wardrobe? Do I need any new clothes? Do you?

I am sorting my wardrobe today. What are you wearing?

Prayer: Loving God, through your Son we learn to give ourselves in service. Thank you for the persons in our time who have had the courage and faith to give their lives in service. Be with us as we realize that Christian living is Christian giving. Help us to remember that what we have or do not have in our wardrobes is not what is most important in our lives. Clothe us in garments that speak of discipleship in whatever roles we find ourselves. Amen.

Part of the Flock

Read Psalm 23.

This familiar Scripture is heard and repeated so often that sometimes we fail to see its deeper meaning. Our inability to find another layer of truth in the psalm is compounded by our common understanding of the word *want*. For most of us, *want* is a synonym for "desire." We give our children what they need, but not everything they want. In the psalm, the word *want* refers to what we need. Read the psalm again with this understanding of the word *want* in mind.

My sister Carol has a flock of sheep. As shepherdess, Carol provides for the needs of her sheep. They cannot open gates to change pastures, cannot fill their troughs with food and water. Neither the ewes nor the rams can build a shed to protect themselves against the storms and cold during lambing season. Without their shepherdess, Carol's sheep would perish. Carol's sheep have their needs met, but sometimes it does appear that they also have desires. Some desire to try the grass beyond the fence. Some desire more than their share at the feeding trough.

It is difficult for us to believe that our Lord is our shepherd and cares as much for us as Carol does for her flock. The abundance of the earth is for our nourishment and enjoyment. The Shepherd provides the resources for the basic necessities of life: food, water, and shelter. Everything we need is provided. When we acknowledge our dependence by repeating, "The Lord is my shepherd," we are making a powerful statement of faith. How much of our anxiety could be prevented if we lived that statement! We say those words, read those words, and think we believe those words—yet, many times our actions indicate the contrary.

Check your credit card statements and your check stubs. Scrutinize your calendar. What or who gets the most attention and/or money? How much time, effort, and resources go for needs? How much for wants or desires? What criteria do you use in defining needs and wants?

I find that separating my needs and my wants into separate categories is not easy. After all, beauty in the form of music and the arts is considered a necessity for fullness of life. Company and school dress codes require certain standards. Unkempt personal appearance diminishes credibility. When we do manage to make progress in separating needs from wants in our lives, the thought that we deserve something more sneaks into our minds. We are told to spend to keep our nation's economy healthy. How much do we need to spend to keep our communities economically healthy? How much can we spend on our wants and remain true to our calling as followers of Christ? The answer seems to be hidden beneath layers of cultural expectations. Yet, we must continue to search for the answer, regardless of the pressures of our society.

Carol's sheep trust her to provide for their needs. God has provided the resources to meet our needs and the needs of those around us. If we are followers of Christ, we have no choice but to care for and to share the bounty of the earth, for Christ shepherds a big flock. It includes all the men, women, and children of our world. The Lord is my shepherd, and the Lord is your shepherd. We are all in the same flock. And we shall not lack our basic needs.

Prayer: Generous Shepherd of us all, we are ever thankful for your presence throughout our lives. Remind us that you have supplied our earth with all that is necessary to meet our needs and even more. Help us to care for and share those resources that all of us, rich and poor, old and young, might live fruitful lives free from hunger and fear. Amen.

Can You Spare a Dime?

Read Matthew 23:23–24 and Malachi 3:8–10.

"How many times have I told you to …?" Parents know that it takes many repetitions before a request to their children seems to sink in. Tithing (giving ten percent, a dime out of every dollar of income, to the church) is mentioned many times in the Bible. For many adult Christians, the request still has not sunk in. If we have listened to those tithing Scriptures, we rationalize our way through our budgeting until the closest we come to tithing is a tenth of what is left over at the end of each pay period. Or we interpret this reading from Matthew to mean that tithing is not really important, that living righteously somehow takes its place.

As a couple, our own journey in Christian stewardship of our finances has been marked by an increasing awareness of the need to take seriously all of the words of Christ reflected in Matthew 23:23, not just the phrases that are most appealing. When we were newlyweds, we sponsored a church youth group and gave regularly to the church budget. We did not tithe. We both came from good Christian homes, but neither one of us had a background of tithing. Then with a new baby, new crib, new card table and chairs, and mattress and sofa from the local Goodwill store, we moved into an apartment in a federal housing project while Wayne attended watch-making school. We continued to support the church with our attendance and gifts, but we did not tithe. We did not even consider that the command to tithe applied to us. We did give those small amounts to the church that we thought were possible to spare from our budget. We also gave small amounts to other charities in addition to the local church.

During those early years of our marriage, we could understand our friends and relatives when they would say that they could not afford to give at present, but when they had enough funds, they would give significant amounts, maybe even big impressive gifts. Sadly, we have yet to see the names of many of those friends and relatives on any donor lists even today. The time when they had enough seems to have never arrived. They are like most of us; the more we have, the more we want. Defining "enough" becomes more and more difficult.

Many churches today stress proportional giving, by which they mean giving in proportion to the amount of your income and the amount necessary to meet your basic needs. I think in our Scripture reading, Jesus was referring to proportional giving. Tithing was to be practiced, but that alone is not enough. To live faithfully, we must obey all the important teachings of the Law. We need to consider justice, mercy, and honesty in determining the amount of our financial giving. Tithing is a minimum amount that for many of us is not enough. Since all we have is from God, we are merely giving back, whether we give proportionally or tithe.

How do we determine how much to give? Some people tithe even when facing financial crises. Others decide that they cannot tithe from their limited incomes. How a tithe is determined varies widely. Is a tithe ten percent of gross income or of net income? Is it before or after taxes? If you are self-employed and income is uncertain, how do you determine the amount of your church pledge? If we gave proportionally when we had very little, shouldn't we give that same way when we have much? Have we ever given sacrificially? For us, giving proportionally seems to be the only faithful way to respond to Jesus' message found in Matthew 23:23.

Years ago we had a visitor in our home who with his wife had determined how much money was necessary to enable them to live modestly. All income above that level was given away. We cannot claim that level of giving. Looking at our home and ability to travel, our crowded closets, the "stuff" that we have accumulated, we must acknowledge that we live above the modest level. Yet, our visitor's example of stewardship has stayed with us as we determine our giving today. Our greatest joys have come when our annual giving equaled our personal spending. Some Christians have known the joy of giving far beyond that amount.

Neither tithing nor proportional giving is a ticket into

heaven. Being rich or being poor does not determine the worth of an individual in God's eyes. Grace is not earned with dollars.

What amount do you give back to God? Your answer is between you and God.

Prayer: Generous God, we confess that we find it difficult to practice generosity. We like having enough money. We like the material riches that money can buy. We rationalize our own meager offerings and expect others to give generously. Forgive our greedy, self-centered lifestyles. Let us never forget your graciousness to us. Help us to practice sacrificial giving as well as servant living. Amen.

A Litany of Faith

Read 1 Corinthians 1.

When I studied Paul's letters to the Corinthians, I found myself becoming discouraged. Our present society seems to have too many parallels to the church in Corinth. However, I was reassured when I read J. Paul Sampley's reflections on 1 Corinthians in *The New Interpreter's Bible.* He noted one theme [the main theme?] of Paul's letters: faith rests in the power of God's grace. Paul scolds and shames, praises and prays. Yet, Sampley points out, every letter of Paul's opens and closes with a statement of God's grace. Paul constantly reminds the Christians of Corinth and us that we cannot minister to others, help others heal, or offer reconciliation unless we first come humbly to the Lord. We cannot give what we do not have ourselves. We must remember whose we are. I offer this litany as a reminder of this fact.

Faith rests in the power of God's grace.
Faith does not rest in the wisdom of women or men,
> *but faith rests in the power of God's grace.*

Faith does not rest in the power of the bank account, the credit rating, or the stock market,
> *but faith rests in the power of God's grace.*

A Litany of Faith

Faith does not rest in the power of government,
> *but faith rests in the power of God's grace.*

Faith does not rest in the wisdom of liberals or conservatives, Democrats or Republicans,
> *but faith rests in the power of God's grace.*

Faith does not rest in the wisdom of either your favorite isms and causes or mine,
> *but faith rests in the power of God's grace.*

Faith does not rest in the wisdom of bishops or other high officials of the church,
> *but faith rests in the power of God's grace.*

Faith does not rest in the wisdom of elders or deacons, of lay speakers or any other titled church leaders.
> *but faith rests in the power of God's grace.*

Faith does not rest in the wisdom of independent Bible study groups,
> *but faith rests in the power of God's grace.*
> *We may have confidence in people or things. We may prayerfully discern which causes, political parties, or groups to support, but ultimately our faith can rest only in the power of God's grace.*

Faith rests in the power of God's grace.

Prayer: O Lord, we know that you alone are God, but it is so easy to fill our hearts with little gods. Forgive us when we put our faith in power, things, ideologies, or people. Encourage us when we are disappointed and when we become cynical and discouraged. Keep us always aware of your glory and the power of your grace. Amen.

Glorify God in Your Body

Read 1 Corinthians 6:19–20.

When I was a teenager, my pastor's wife gave me those verses from 1 Corinthians to put on my mirror. When I moved away from my childhood home, I took those words with me in my heart and mind.

Remembering this Scripture through the years, I have tried to keep my body as healthy as possible. I have not always done a good job. My natural inclination is to spend my days in relatively passive activities such as reading, sewing, and writing. I do enjoy walking and gardening. I do try to eat healthy meals. My body does not qualify as a picture of strength and health.

I do not pretend to speak for everyone with some sort of chronic physical challenge. My symptoms are mild compared to those of many others who suffer with chronic illness. I was diagnosed with multiple sclerosis at the age of forty-seven. Three years later, I survived a tragic accident, which added to my physical challenges. I have a high level of function and lead a normal life, but I never forget my uninvited permanent guests. The pesky everyday symptoms—primarily fatigue, pain, and impaired balance—vary in intensity. They remind me that I am not alone in this body. My family has been immensely supportive, helpful, and loving. For all of us, frustration is frequently a part of the day.

Many people have chronic illnesses. Some of those illnesses are almost invisible. We take medications to deal with the symptoms, use whatever aids for living that are necessary, and live fruitful lives. All of us, with or without challenges, can run the race of life to the best of our abilities. Living with integrity and with respect for our bodies and for the bodies of others is also living with respect for God.

Each of us is more than a disease or a handicapping condition. I am more than a survivor of an accident, more than someone with a chronic disease. You are not Mrs. Arthritis or Mr. Parkinson. I am myself, and you are yourself; we are persons who just happen to have arthritis or Parkinson's disease or multiple sclerosis or some other challenge.

We glorify God in our bodies by accepting help from others when we need it. Accepting help allows others to have the joy of giving and serving. Our culture values self-reliance to the extreme. Pride in "doing it myself" is expected and celebrated. We are to be tough and strong, able to do things for ourselves. Yet, those very characteristics can keep us from God by helping us deny our need for God. The gift of chronic illness can mean coming to God in pain and discouragement, acknowledging that we are helpless without the Comforter. In fact, many of the heroes of the faith, in the Bible and throughout history, have been those with physical illnesses or impediments.

Chronic illness makes us realize that we cannot do it alone. For some, illness literally means that even the basics of life are not done alone. For those children of God, their daily caregivers glorify God in their acts of physical, emotional, and spiritual support. The rest of us, who have no idea of the daily challenges they face, can offer ourselves to be used in any way possible that is beneficial in meeting needs.

Chronic illness may or may not lead to increased patience on the part of the caregiver or on the part of the person who is suffering. Chronic illness sometimes leads to bitterness. We all know righteous persons who suffer way beyond what we might consider "fair." Chronic illness is not punishment; it just is.

Keeping the words of this Scripture in our hearts and practicing these words can be difficult for the strong as well as the weak. The temptations to glorify self and not God loom large for those who excel physically. If you are fortunate enough to have a strong body, do what you can to keep it that way. Do not waste the gift given you. Rejoice in muscles that are strong and responsive. Spend your strength carefully. Join with others in healthy exercise, not with an air of superiority, but with the aim to keep your body strong and healthy as long as possible, that you may glorify God in your body.

Through all of life, for both the strong and the weak, it helps to remember that nowhere in Scripture do we read that physical strength is necessary for salvation or to receive the grace of God. Neither great physical strength nor great physical weakness signifies great favor with God. Robust health and strength do not necessarily indicate righteousness. Chronic illness does not automatically indicate sin or moral weakness. Having a chronic illness does not mean being chosen for special testing or witness. Unique opportunities for witness and service are open for both the healthy and the weak children of God. The Spirit of God descends on healthy and stricken bodies and hearts alike.

Glorify God in your body. Your body is a gift to be treasured. You might not have the body you wish for, but you always have God's spirit with you and within you.

Prayer: Loving God, we come to you, sometimes broken in body and sometimes broken in spirit. Life is not always easy. We lose our sense of priorities. We become frustrated with ourselves and with those around us. Give us strength, patience, and courage. Remind us who we will always be, regardless of the challenges we face. Remind us that we are your children and recipients of your love, presence, and comfort. Amen.

Just Plain Folks

Read Exodus 18:13–27 and Matthew 10:1–4.

Heads bent over papers, and pencils scratched the relevant boxes. Another group of church leaders were identifying their leadership styles. Some of us are naturally loners. Some of us have well-developed independent streaks and prefer "going it alone." We might feel that asking others to help us takes too much time. We might want to be certain the project is done the correct way (our way). Some of us prefer to lead quietly behind the scenes.

One thing the Bible makes clear is that every leader needs helpers. Moses could not do everything by himself. He was wearing himself out. He finally took the advice of his father-in-law Jethro and chose capable men to help him. He appointed leaders of thousands, hundreds, fifties, and tens. Moses may have had the first organizational chart of the church. Even Jesus did not attempt to accomplish his ministry alone, but chose twelve apostles. The twelve came from varied backgrounds; none were synagogue officials or priests from the tribe of Aaron. Their peers probably considered the apostles just plain folks.

Most churches today follow the example of Moses and have some sort of organizational chart of leadership. Some are quite formal and detailed, while others are informal and unstructured. Most churches make some distinction between the clergy or trained church leaders and the laity.

I admire the education and dedication of the clergy. In spite of what I know from my study of Scripture, I have at times made the excuse for my lack of action that I am only a layperson. Then I am reminded that those who are not ordained clergy are never just laypeople. Each layperson is responsible for the ministry of the church just as surely as the clergy. Both clergy and laity are called and gifted by God. Calls and gifts are not determined by titles. We leave the ministry of the church to professionals at the peril of our congregations. Our churches exist neither for the sake of employment opportunities for the clergy nor for the relief of servant responsibilities for the laity. The church exists that both clergy and laity might be nurtured through worship and fellowship, and enabled to go forth in service and witness to a world hungry for the Word and the love of God. Each of us may at some point be the only way someone experiences Christian faith in action.

The majority of the people called by Christ were probably just plain folks. Most did not walk around in long costly robes or have reserved seats in the synagogues. Jesus was born to plain folks who listened to God. Plain people were and are chosen by God, brothers and sisters in Christ, each responding to God's particular call for his or her unique role.

Prayer: Remind us, O God, that each of us is precious in your sight and worthy of serving you. Help us to develop and use our own talents and to enable others to develop and use their talents in your service. Remind us that none of us are *just* plain folks. Amen.

Original Condition

Read John 3:3–10.

On the top shelf in our family room, my last doll Betsy sits beside a metal toy truck, a favorite childhood toy belonging to my husband. Betsy's hair is thin and has lost its original curl from frequent shampoos and sets. The dented metal truck has one wheel missing. The original gift boxes that held the toys fresh from Santa's bag disappeared long ago. We value the toys as sentimental reminders of our family history.

According to the information given to collectors who bring items for appraisals to television antique shows, old toys in original, mint condition in pristine boxes sell for the highest prices at auctions. An antique dealer would not be impressed with my Betsy doll or with my husband's old toy truck. Yet, toys are intended for play. Dolls and stuffed toys share naps and nights with their small owners, ride along to Grandma and Grandpa's house, and sometimes float in bathtub bubbles. Toy trucks carry blocks, stones, candy, and dry cereal. Children crash toy trucks and cars into baseboards inside the house and lose toys in the bushes on the lawn. Fortunately for the children who own them, most toys do not remain in their original condition.

My husband and I are at what some might term antique ages. We are not in our original condition. Humans do not remain in their original condition if they live past birth. Everyone gains weight and height. The physical changes as we age are undeniable no matter how much we might attempt to delay them. Our culture values the appearance of youth. Full-page newspaper advertisements feature products that promise to make us look decades younger.

The Bible makes no such promises. If we confess Christ and become his followers, life is not supposed to remain the same. Christians are intended to live their faith. According to what we study in Scripture, we can expect some wear and tear. Ending life in our original physical or spiritual condition is not an option for Christians.

What would be the appraised value of our lives as Christians, antique or not? What are the signs that we have lived as Christians? What is the evidence of the loads we have carried for others? Are there cheeks streaked with tears of compassion, worry lines from bedside vigils, or pricked fingers from gathering roses for a grieving and lonely widow? Are our feet blistered from walking miles to raise funds for the least of these? Where are the laugh lines from shared times with family and friends? What about our spiritual condition? Has our faith matured with our bodies, or is it still in the primary school stage? What evidence of aging as Christians do we exhibit?

Regardless of your current age, young or antique, is your Christian life still sealed in its mint condition baptismal box, waiting to be opened and used? How would you appraise your life as a Christian?

Prayer: Creator God, we are most fully human when we honor our creation in your image. Be with us through the ages and stages of our lives. Thank you for the wonderful opportunities given us to experience the joy and sadness of our earthly lives. Help us to live in witness and in praise, in service and even in sacrifice. Amen.

Pin Drop

Read Psalm 46:10.

As the clock crept closer to dismissal time, we squirmed in anticipation and shuffled our feet under our desks. The older boys whispered plans for a race after school. The upper-grade girls giggled softly. Miss Virginia rapped on her teacher's desk for quiet with limited response. Picking up a large straight pin, she told us that as soon as we could hear the pin hit the floor when she dropped it behind the upright piano, school would be dismissed. Our feet suddenly became still and silent. The whispering and giggling stopped. We held our breath as we strained to hear the faint sound of the pin on the hardwood floor. There. We heard it!

The pin drop became an exercise we all enjoyed. We learned to listen intently. Our teacher had found an effective way to get our attention.

Listening closely to others is difficult for many of us. How many times have I wished for the speaker to finish so that I might speak my thoughts? My ability to listen intently for an extended length of time is frequently limited. My mind wanders. I begin to mentally make lists of things to do. Or the speaker triggers a reverie on a completely unrelated subject.

So it is with listening for God. We long for God's

word to lead us. We long for relief from conflict within our families or congregations. We honestly seek God's guidance in our daily lives. With our problems given to God, we leave our prayer time eager for our desired results. Our minds race with the clutter and clatter of our own preferred solutions. We ask God again and again for help. We read all of the latest self-help books. We think that we have tried everything. The noise of our activity drowns out God's still small voice. We are so busy with the problems that we are unable to hear the answers. In a hymn Septimus Winner wrote in 1868, he knew "Whispering Hope." To hear a whisper "soft as an angel's voice," to have hope, we must be quiet and listen.

Listening is an integral part of prayer that is frequently forgotten. In fact, sometimes listening is all of prayer. I need to remember the lesson I learned in that schoolroom long ago. I need to quiet my soul and listen so intently that I can hear a pin drop.

Prayer: Lord of many voices, speak to us as we pray. We long to hear your voice. Remind us to listen quietly, to be still, and to know that you are God. Amen.

Vision

Read Acts 16:6–10.

Several years ago, the organized women in our denomination had as their theme and challenge, "Make Plain the Vision." Local congregations are urged to write their own vision statements. In Bible study and prayer groups, individuals are encouraged to write vision statements. The goal is for individuals and groups to focus on their purpose for being. The first difficulty is defining the exact meaning that the word *vision* has for Christians. The second challenge is determining that vision for the individual or group. Perhaps a childhood experience of mine might help us with both tasks.

I had my first visit to the optometrist when I was ten years old. The belated visit came at the urging of the county health nurse who visited our one room school. My father took me to the neighboring town of Atchison and left me at the optometrist's office with instructions to go to my grandparents' house after the examination. The wall chart of letters was easily read with my left eye, but with the right eye, the chart was blurred and partially black. Numerous lenses were tried. My eyes were dilated. Try as I might, I could not change the performance of my right eye.

The doctor scolded me. "That is a lazy eye; you can

see with it if you try." I had never been called lazy before. I was crushed at being held accountable for something beyond my control. I left the office in shame.

The world was blurry, and the light hurt my eyes. The doctor had not explained that the muscles of my eyes were temporarily paralyzed, resulting in sensitivity to light and my vision being out of focus. At the soda fountain, I could not distinguish the coins to pay for my treat. When I got on the city bus, the driver had to take the appropriate number of coins from my hand. The bright sunlight hurt my eyes. I was certain everyone considered me a stupid, lazy country girl.

"Where are you going?" the driver asked.

"To Grandma Moore's," I replied.

Passengers snickered, and the driver smiled. It had not occurred to my parents that I did not know the street address of my grandparents' home. Further questioning from the bus driver resulted in my giving him a fairly accurate description of their neighborhood. He was able to determine where I needed to go. He helped me with a bus transfer, and I soon arrived safely at Grandma's house, where she waited on the front porch swing. My vision was clearer, and I easily recognized the house and Grandma.

Like most children with poor vision, I was unaware that I did not see as well as I should. To gain that knowledge and change the situation, I had endured an uncomfortable examination and suffered at the hands of an insensitive professional. My encounters with optometrists since then have been very positive. Then I felt helpless to arrive at a positive outcome. I did not know my destination, but I encountered a helpful guide. I saw the world blurred and without focus, yet I finally arrived safely at my grandparents' home.

Sometimes our individual and corporate spiritual lives are like my childhood visual experience. We fail to realize how much our vision is limited. We are unable to grasp our Christian vision because our own muscles of faith, receptiveness, and courage are temporarily paralyzed. We need a visual examination and corrective lenses. Others might wound us. Seeing the world in a new light with a new awareness of God's vision for us might cause us to experience a temporary paralysis of faith. Seeing a blurred world is less demanding. We retreat to a dark closet, pray, wait, and listen. Coming out of that dark closet, we can focus more clearly.

God gives us visions. Would you and I recognize a vision if we saw one? By studying Scripture and Biblical commentary, we gain insight into what characterizes a vision. In the Bible, we learn that God gave visions to individuals. The vision to each was specifically matched to the unique gift and unique world need that the gift could fulfill. The vision to each was given to the heart not the mind. Individuals then shared their visions with friends and strangers.

What is it in your experience of Christ that the world needs you to share? Answering that question might require more time alone with God. It might mean changing lenses again and again as you grow in faith.

Sometimes seeing the world through the new lenses of a vision means giving up old habits. Sometimes recognizing our vision changes the direction of our lives completely. Our visions might be positively received in unexpected places. There will be those who are very helpful and those who belittle us. Our visions might not make any sense to the world, but receiving our visions makes our hearts sing. Sharing our visions is a joyous experience. The Holy Spirit is at work in earthly vessels.

Prayer: O God, you speak to us in so many ways. Help us to listen and look, that we might hear and see the vision you have for us. Be with us as we share that vision with joy and enthusiasm. Amen.

Emergency Lighting

Read John 8:12.

I remember how delighted I was as a small child on the farm when we were first able to flip a switch or pull a chain and have light. We could have light in every room when we needed it, without the hazards of carrying oil lamps from room to room. The yard light was especially wonderful. No more danger of using lanterns to check on livestock or make other trips outside at night. We were able to look across the bottomlands to our neighbors' farms and note when their yard lights went on and off, signaling that all was well with them or that there might be an emergency. Later I learned that my father had been instrumental in forming the first rural electric cooperative in Kansas.

Our children remember lanterns used only on camping adventures or during power failures. Their flashlights by their bedsides revealed cats posing as monsters under the beds.

Emergency lighting is appreciated by people of all ages. Whether our emergency lights are oil lamps, lanterns, or flashlights, light is not available unless we have fuel or batteries. Stumbling and fumbling in the dark for fresh batteries is frustrating and dangerous. Filling an oil lamp by candlelight is even more so. It is important to keep the lamps filled and the batteries charged.

Spiritual darkness can come to us even in broad daylight when a crisis catches and covers us like a black moonless night. Even giants of the faith have endured that darkness of the spirit. There is no easy switch to turn on a light in such a crisis and no automatic sensor to light the way. We must rely on our spiritual emergency lighting. In the midst of a crisis, it is difficult or impossible to recharge run-down faith batteries. It is then that we depend on fully charged spiritual batteries—batteries charged not only by ourselves, but also by others with their prayers and presence. Alone, we lack the power to recharge those batteries. Only through the recharging of prayer and faithful living can we be ready for whatever life brings. The amount of charge in our spiritual batteries can mean the difference between despair and hope. Just as faith the size of a mustard seed can move mountains, so even a tiny light can carry us through long dark passages safely. The journey may be short or long. It may require several batteries. If we keep the light of Christ ahead, the dark shadows will eventually stretch behind us.

Prayer: Dear Creator God, nudge us into the night with our batteries fully charged. We confess that when life is going along smoothly without mishap, we become self-centered and forget how weak our own power source is. Remind us to keep connected to you, our strength and light. Grant us the wisdom to always be ready for the inevitable crises in our lives. Empower us, O God, to share your light with others. Amen.

Part 5

Traveling Through the Christian Year

God does not need the seasons of the Christian year—
Advent, Christmastide, Ordinary Time, Lent, Easter,
Pentecost, and Ordinary Time (or Kingdomtide)—to be
God. Neither does God need our many specially designated
Sundays to be God. Most of our markers in the liturgical
year are not even mentioned in the Bible, and some
were not celebrated until very recent times. Some of our
celebrations are transformations of pagan festivals. The
dates that have been chosen may have little relevance to the
dates of the actual birth and crucifixion of Christ or other
Biblical events. God is not confined by our calendars.

The Christian liturgical calendar is helpful to us because
from our births we are shaped by calendars and seasons,
celebrations and sorrows. We go through the cycles of the
twelve months and the four seasons again and again. Each
year is the same and yet different. Just as our physical
lives are framed by calendars and seasons, our spiritual
lives are framed by the Christian year. The seasons of the
Christian year remind us of prophets and messengers, of
faithful people journeying with God through the ages.
We are reminded of Christ's birth, ministry, crucifixion,
resurrection, and promise to come again. Celebrating

Pentecost, we are reminded that God is with us in every season. These meditations represent some of my own travels through the Christian year.

Advent

An increasing number of Christian families are observing Advent by lighting Advent candles in their homes or having special family devotions during this season between Thanksgiving and Christmas. Such observances help to emphasize the religious meaning of Christmas while still taking part in the secular traditions of the holiday season. Joyous celebrations are surely welcomed by God. How can we help but celebrate the promises of Advent?

One Candle

Read Luke 1:46–55.

Each morning during the winter, we have a light parade at our house—first the lamps at the head of the bed, then the bathroom light, the kitchen light, and the dining room light. Instant light is a perk of our modern age and a major safety tool with a dark cat in the house. We are thankful for light to help us go about our business in the morning darkness.

During Advent, we reverse the light parade by turning out the lights as we prepare for our morning devotions. Outside the windows, we see the stars in the dark sky. In the dark dining room, we find our chairs and light the first candle of the Advent wreath. With the light of that single candle, we read Scripture and devotions and eat our meal. Each week, we light another candle, and so each successive week of Advent, it becomes easier to read the Scripture and devotions and easier to eat our meal.

We decided to do this as a symbol of the Light coming into the world and driving out darkness. Each morning in that first week of Advent, we are made aware of the power of one candle. You can read by the light of one candle. You can find your plate, cup, and bowl. Two candles make it easier to see, three easier still, and the four candles in the fourth week of Advent make our table seem bright.

One Candle

Mary was one little candle. God chose this very young woman to be the mother of Christ. Throughout history, one person has often made the difference—one person who made the discovery in science and health, one person who first spoke out against social injustice, and one person who finally refused to give up her seat on the bus. We know the power of one, and yet we sometimes forget. The nativity story is our reminder.

Mary visited one older relative, Elizabeth, who was also pregnant. This one old woman gave Mary love and insight. This one old woman was her mentor.

As mothers, we are aware of the oneness of the experience of childbirth. In the stable or in the delivery room, one woman is actually giving birth, no matter how many doctors and nurses, family and midwives, or husbands might be assisting.

One husband. Did Joseph have a candle there in the stable, or a small oil lamp? Did he hold it close to see the baby for the first time?

One baby, one candle—even one candle—drives away the darkness. Two candles, three candles, four candles, then endless candles circling sanctuaries and continents, in huts and hovels, condos and castles, the candlepower growing through the centuries, life after life reflecting the Light of life.

So we come to Christ one at a time, completely dependent upon God's grace. Each of us is like that first single candle burning in the morning darkness. One at a time we live our lives, giving light, sharing Christ's light.

How many other candles will you light? What darkness will your candle drive away? What Scripture will it illuminate? What food will it reveal?

Prayer: Lord, we come to you one at a time, each like a single candle, each with a beautiful form and light to share. Remind us of the beauty of each single candle. Remind us of the power of each candle and the even greater power of many candles. Be with us in this Advent as we come to you, one at a time, our candles burning, empowered by your love. Amen.

Gifts for the Meantime

Read Isaiah 40:3–5 and Mark 1:1–3.

I love Christmas. I collect gifts for family and friends all year long, decorate until Christmas Eve, and generally enjoy the four weeks preceding Christmas that we call Advent. When our children were young, we had to remind them daily that Christmas would come and, in the meantime, they must be patient.

In our world of instant gratification, we seldom use the phrase "in the meantime," which means making do until the time when what we really want can be obtained or enjoyed. It requires making decisions that will enable the desired future goal. Advent can be a time when we are particularly aware that we live in the meantime, between the already happened and the not yet.

Advent is a reminder that we are living in a time of preparation for the Second Coming, as our communion liturgy indicates when we repeat the great mystery of faith: *Christ has died; Christ is risen; Christ will come again.* And in the meantime, come with me through Advent.

A stack of presents waits for me under the tree. I will open one just before my evening quiet time each week of Advent. I choose the first gift to unwrap. It is marked with a fragile tag, so I unwrap carefully. Inside is a small mirror. A planned glance in my mirror usually results in a

161

little retouching in my mind, but this glance is unexpected and unaltered. When I see my reflection, I am surprised. This woman looks tired and overburdened. There is too much to do and so little time. My reflection in the mirror is partly the result of my genes and other conditions beyond my control. Yet much of what I see is the result of my own cumulative decisions.

So it is with Advent. My reflection in the mirror, my daily schedule, and the tenor of my Advent will be determined by the choices I make. I need to carefully evaluate my own expectations of what must be accomplished in these weeks before Christmas. Priorities must be determined, taking into account my energy and time restraints. What is necessary for me to make this Advent a holy season for myself and for my family? What must I do to change that reflection in my mirror to one of anticipation and joyful preparation?

The package I choose to open the second week has the wrapping torn, a corner of the box crumpled. The package was obviously poorly prepared for shipping. When I open it, I am delighted to find a little earthenware teapot. It is the handwork of an artist. But the handle is broken, and the pot is cracked in several places. It is probably useless. I am disappointed.

Sitting quietly by the fire, I think of the times that I have not been properly prepared. Can I ever be prepared for this Christmas let alone be prepared for when Christ comes again? I must be intentional. I must take time.

In this meantime of Advent, I must live as though Christ will be here for supper, even if it is soup. It will take time to mend relationships as damaged as the teapot. Gathering up the wrappings, I remember that we are all living in "earthen vessels" and most of us in cracked vessels. On my own, I will never be ready. God's power and love, not our own flawed efforts, enable each of us to prepare for the meantimes of our lives.

My to-do list is not any shorter and another week has passed. It is time to open a gift. I choose one that I think I especially deserve after my week of frantic activity. This one looks like it came from my favorite upscale store. Maybe it is that blouse I have seen in the dress shop window. With great anticipation, I unwrap the gift, saving the fancy bow and wrapping paper. I unfold the fine tissue paper to find … an apron, a plain, serviceable apron! Rather deceptive packaging, I think. It seems a cruel trick. It is not at all what I expected from the wrapping.

Sometimes, to hide the real contents, I have intentionally wrapped a package to look like something it was not—a tiny box inside a larger one, inside a larger one, like Russian dolls one inside the other. I intend it all in fun. Somehow, this does not seem funny. Tying the plain little apron over my robe, I fix a cup of tea and find a quiet corner. Then it comes to me.

What sort of deceptive wrapping am I wearing this Advent? Has my frantic activity been a wrapping to hide the real me? The apron on my lap catches a drop of tea. That plain, simple apron now strangely gives a sense of comfort. As my mother lovingly tied an apron around me when I helped her with Christmas baking, this apron reminds me that I am a loved child of God. I am a plain, loved child serving with my Parent in the meantime of Advent.

This fourth week of Advent, I very carefully choose the gift to open; at this point, I am leery of surprises. Inside this simply wrapped package, I find the gift that I have coveted for years. The emerald and diamond pendant on a gold chain is even lovelier than I had envisioned—lovely and very, very expensive. The purchase price must have meant great sacrifice. Instead of rejoicing, I feel guilty. I think the gift is far too extravagant, too precious. I really do not deserve this gift.

During this Advent meantime, I seem unable to escape layers of meaning in the layers of gift-wrap. So with this gift I remember examples of costly gifts in the Scriptures. I remember the greatest Gift of all—a Gift purchased with great sacrifice, a Gift undeserved.

Who am I to reject a gift because I did not earn it or deserve it? None of us deserve the grace of Christ. None of us earn grace. It is a *gift*. Gifts are unearned.

A mirror, a cracked teapot, an apron, and an unearned

expensive gift—not the usual symbols of Advent, but significant in terms of gifts for the meantime.

Oh, one more gift catches my attention. See that gift tucked back under the branches. It is wrapped in burlap … does not look too promising … some hay in the folds … a strange presence about it. I am both drawn to that gift and afraid of what opening it might mean. Do I have to wait until Christmas morning? Does it matter when it is opened?

In the meantime …

Prayer: Patient God, forgive us our impatience. Waiting is difficult for us. To discern what is most important in our lives sometimes seems impossible. We fret over small things and neglect to see the large picture. We have difficulty remembering the difference between needs and wants. We hurry and fret and forget to enjoy the moments of our lives. Generous God, remind us to always accept with joy and thanksgiving those gifts given in love, regardless of the monetary value. In this Advent, help us to remember the greatest Gift of love ever given. Amen.

No-Banana Banana Bread

Read Psalm 146 and Matthew 1:18–23.

When I was a young mother, our most adventuresome toddler presented numerous challenges to my attempts at baking. I had been concentrating on a new recipe when an unusual crunchy sound interrupted an equally unusual quiet. When I turned from studying my cookbook, there stood our toddler, stuck proudly in the middle of her mixture of syrup and cereal with her sweetly encrusted hands raised in the classic signal to be picked up. I longed, just for a moment, for the time when I could bake without such distractions. I assumed that when I reached the empty-nest stage, my undivided attention would result in culinary masterpieces.

With the syrup and cereal episode now decades past, such a time had finally arrived. Banana bread would not be an exotic addition to the church brunch menu, but good banana bread was always welcomed. I carefully measured the ingredients and basked in my efficiency as I ground the nuts with the top mixer attachment while the beater below creamed the margarine and sugar.

The phone rang. The doorbell chimed. The dryer buzzed. No problem. I was a survivor of years of interruptions. I added the rest of the ingredients plus a bit of lemon juice to the batter to make it especially light, poured the just-

166

right batter into the pan, and put the pan into the oven. It was time to wash the bowls.

On the flour-dusted counter sat the bowl of mashed and measured bananas! I had made no-banana banana bread!

The essential ingredients for a quick bread were in the pan, so the final product was different, but very good. The texture was a lot like pound cake and made a delicious foundation for cheese spreads. Folks even asked for the recipe.

Sometimes Christmas is like that. We are anticipating a near perfect holiday. Everything is laid out in readiness. Then, something happens. Circumstances are changed. The changes can be as small as a decoration missing or broken. Changes can be overwhelming. Trust and love are shattered like broken Christmas balls as someone breaks from the family. Perhaps, someone very dear has died and only memories fill the limp stocking on the mantle.

Christmas will be different. It can be good. The essential ingredient of Christmas—God's loving us enough to come wrapped in swaddling clothes in a manger—is still true. Think of it, a vulnerable baby, God in the flesh! Born to common parents! God with *us*! God with us then, and God with us now. No matter what else is different at our Christmas, the essential ingredient—the Gift of love—is always there, waiting to be opened. We can absolutely count on it.

We sing, very softly, with the angels. Someday we will once again rejoice and be glad.

Prayer: O God, thank you for the great gift of your love that comes to us and remains with us. Help us to remember, even in the midst of our interruptions, busyness, and brokenness, that you keep your promises to your people. Grant us calm, peace, and joy at this Advent and Christmas season. Amen.

Please, Touch

Read Luke 18:15–17 and John 1:14.

In the twilight, the glass ornaments handed down through generations reflect the twinkling lights draped on the branches of the Christmas tree. Great-grandmother's delicately painted blown-glass angel keeps watch from on high. Grandpa's faded red Santa hangs crookedly from its hook on a lower branch. Swaying gently, a cherished reindeer with a red nose blinks its light in counterpoint to the ringing of the tiny bells around its collar.

"Don't you dare touch!" exclaims a nervous mother.

"Stay away," adds a tired father, as the starry-eyed young child moves closer to the tree.

The nativity set is carefully arranged on the buffet. Candles cast a soft glow on the finely carved figures. The baby Jesus figure, plump and smiling, is nestled in the manger. The little lamb lies peacefully by the lion. A shepherd stands guard at the stable entrance.

"Don't touch that baby!"

"Put that shepherd down!"

The parental admonitions are loud and strong. The starry eyes of their child glisten with tears.

Understandable cautions from the parents, and yet Christmas is for touching. Let's take a moment to reflect on the message we are giving to children when the words they hear most often during the season are "Don't touch."

Perhaps the innkeeper asked, "May I hold the baby? So tiny! I can hardly believe he's real."

Joseph may have exclaimed, "Look, he's holding onto my finger!"

God became flesh and dwelt among us. Please, touch, for with Christmas, *God became touchable*. Christmas is about touching and holding that which is loved above all else.

"Please, touch," God says to us. "Please, touch the branches of my tree; feel the soft needles and smell the fragrance. Please, touch my snowflakes settling softly on your hair. Please, touch the garlands lining the windowsill. Stroke the wrinkled cheek of your grandmother. Pat the soft hand of the baby. Grasp the sticky hand of the toddler, the ringed hand of your sister, and your grandfather's calloused fingers. Place your hand in your loved one's hand and walk together. Gently place a warm coat on the shoulders of the homeless man shivering on the street corner. Put a toy into the hand of the little child watching at the window for a Santa that never comes. Wipe away with love the tear, glistening grief on the cheek of someone mourning a loved one. Shake the hand of the moneylender, and give the gift of Good News."

Christmas is for touching. At Christmas, God became touchable.

Prayer: O Christ, God become flesh, open our hearts to the deeper meaning of your birth that we might celebrate your gift to us. Help us to make this Christmas touchable for all of your children. Amen.

Christmas Clothes

Read Colossians 3:12–17.

My sewing machine went at full speed while the vacuum cleaner stayed in the closet. It was time to make new dresses for our daughters for the grade school Christmas carol program to be held at our community building. Hundreds of children perched on the bleachers with their classmates would form a community Christmas card—little boys with scrubbed faces, combed hair, and new shirts (mostly tucked in neatly) and little girls in their red Christmas dresses. The children sang Christmas songs to their parents, other proud relatives, and friends.

That living Christmas card is no longer held. The event was a major commitment of time and endeavor not only for the students but also for the teachers. When the program was discontinued, some of the teachers heaved sighs of relief, but for many in the community, a true celebration of Christmas was greatly missed.

Still, brightly colored clothes for Christmas reflect the joyous celebration of the season. And under the Christmas tree, there is almost certain to be at least one sweater or tie.

We do not have snapshots in our Bibles of that first Christmas. We use our imaginations and what historical information is available to costume the players in our

Christmas programs. Christmas cards might depict baby Jesus as a royal prince or as an ordinary baby of many different ethnicities, but Mary almost always wears a blue dress. Whatever the color, it was probably a simple garment of common cloth. Mary and Joseph would have had on their travel clothes, wrinkled and dirty from the journey. We might think that Mary and Joseph were not dressed for the part they were playing in the world. Scripture tells us that Mary wrapped Jesus in bands of cloth. We don't know the details of that humble birth.

Throughout the Old and New Testaments, clothing styles did not change dramatically. Clothing indicated social status and the role in church and society even more sharply than now. Have we missed how astounding it was that God did not clothe the Babe and his parents in royal robes? Have we missed the underlying message that what matters is in the heart? Was God setting a new clothing standard for Christians?

Scripture often uses clothing metaphorically. The writer of Colossians did not mention the first Christmas wardrobe, but he told them to choose clothes made with threads of compassion, kindness, humility, meekness, patience, and above all love.

The writer said, in effect, to imagine each morning that you put on a huge cloak that holds all the qualities of life in the Spirit. This cloak will shape your heart and actions and enable you to live in harmony and unity.

This Christmas put on your new Christmas clothes. Dress your children in their brightest and finest to celebrate the season. Wrap around their hearts and yours a cloak woven with those threads of compassion, kindness, humility, meekness, patience, and love to wear every day of the year. Those clothes will last through the seasons. Those clothes will grow with your children. Those clothes will always be what the fashionable Christian wears.

Prayer: Creator God, thank you for our earthly garments and for the spiritual garments that enable us to better live our days as disciples. Help us to carefully choose and liberally share both. Amen.

Christmastide

At last the big day is here. It comes none too soon for little ones and much too soon for parents. It is Christmas. After the candlelight services on Christmas Eve and the frantic opening of gifts on Christmas morning, the rest of Christmastide may seem somewhat of a letdown. The thought that Christmas might last twelve days is too much for those weary of the many demands of the season. Yet, those twelve days might be just what we need to absorb just how incredible it is that God became one of us.

God Became Man

Read Matthew 1:23 and Luke 2:52.

I have always loved everything about Christmas celebrations. As a child, I watched with wide-eyed wonder when Santa came to our schoolroom. I cherished the nativity sets, carols, and stories in Sunday school. I helped Mom fill our long brown stockings with oranges, homemade fudge, store-bought Christmas candy, and popcorn balls.

As an adult, I came to appreciate more fully the meaning of this lowly birth we celebrate: God became not just with us *but one of us.* I enjoy the many varied images in stories and paintings of that first Christmas. Yet, I wish I had read more stories and seen more paintings that depicted the infant Jesus more realistically. Depictions of the holy family seldom portray normal family life. Paintings of Mary nursing her holy infant existed but were never displayed in our church or home. A picture of Joseph holding the hand of Jesus as a toddler could have helped me realize the miracle of God becoming man.

Step by step, Jesus grew in wisdom and in strength, and God's blessing was upon him. Mary and Joseph must have been good parents, nurturing this child physically, socially, and spiritually to adulthood. Perhaps we would have stronger young Christian families in our congregations and communities if we thought more about that model of parenting. What part did the village play in Jesus' upbringing? Was Jesus treated like any other child in the village? Was he ostracized because of his illegitimate birth? What part did the extended family play? We assume from studies of life in that time that both village and extended family played large roles, but we can only assume. We do know that no child grows into a healthy adult without a lot of help. Do our faith-extended families, our church "villages," enable young parents to raise their children to increase in wisdom, in strength, and in favor with God and man?

Jesus grew and left his parents and siblings. Did his family understand his leaving? The temptations that Jesus faced in the desert as a young man are not unlike those that young people (and adults) face today as they leave the shelter and protection of their families for the first time. Desiring power and fame, taking unnecessary risks to prove favor with God, putting self first, and valuing temporary physical satisfaction ahead of spiritual health are temptations just as real now as they were then. Maybe *how* Jesus resisted temptation shows us that God's love for us humans does not depend on miracles. We can be fully human, with all the wonders and dangers, failures and triumphs of our humanness. Because of Jesus' example, we can trust completely in God's love.

Jesus showed us how to be fully human as children of God. He was always in touch with God. He was praised and criticized, welcomed and rebuffed. He had friends who betrayed him, friends who were fearful, and friends who were faithful. He helped the rich and famous and those on the bottom rungs of society. He suffered, gave his life, and triumphed in the end. And God, his parent, was always with him.

Prayer: Parent God, thank you for the gift of your Son, who showed us how to live, serve, and die secure in your love. Amen.

Rest Stop

Read Matthew 2:13–23.

We welcome few signs on our highways more than those signs indicating a rest area ahead. As tired and sleepy travelers, we stop for a quick nap or a brisk walk, to use the restrooms, to picnic, or to walk the family pet. We listen to the current weather conditions on the road ahead. We check maps to make certain we have the best directions to our destination.

After the hurry and scurry of Advent and Christmas Day, our church calendar gives us the opportunity for just the rest stop we need. The twelve days between Christmas on December 25 and Epiphany on January 6 are designated Christmastide, also known as the Twelve Days of Christmas. Although its origin is unclear, the Twelve Days of Christmas, like many traditions, probably comes from a Roman pagan festival. The interpretation, the time frame, and the traditions observed vary greatly among Christian churches. Using this season as a rest stop gives us the opportunity to look at the current condition of our spiritual lives. We can decide the direction and path necessary to make our dreams come true in the New Year.

What are the current conditions of your spiritual life? What is the best thing that has happened in the past year that could serve as a vehicle for improving your spiritual life in the New Year? What opportunities for Bible study, service, or participation in prayer groups have helped you the most on your journey of discipleship? Did the spirit of generosity at Christmas remind you of opportunities for sharing throughout the year? Are you on a rocky road or a four-lane highway? A detour? What is the level of your commitment? What does the road ahead look like? Unsettled? Stormy? Sunny? Take an honest spiritual inventory of your life, rest, and remember. Begin the journey into the New Year under your best current conditions.

How do we know what direction our lives should take in the New Year? What tools can we use? In our reading from Matthew, we notice dreams, dreams, and more dreams. Not only had God been speaking through dreams to his people for centuries, giving warnings, orders, and reassurances, but God also spoke in dreams to the major players in the Christmas story. God told the Magi in a dream not to report to Herod exactly where the baby Jesus was and to return to their country by a different route. Joseph was told in a dream to flee to Egypt when Herod ordered the slaughter of all infant boys. Joseph was then told in a dream that it was safe to return to Israel because Herod was dead. Joseph was afraid to return because he knew that Archelaus, who had succeeded Herod, was as cruel as his father had been. Finally, Joseph was told in another dream to make his home for his family in Nazareth in the province of Galilee.

When we rest and sleep, we often dream. Most Christians today do not know quite what to make of the idea of God's speaking to us through our dreams. Is hearing God in a dream much like hearing God in prayer? Perhaps we need to practice listening to that still small voice that speaks to us when we are awake or when we are dreaming. Although Joseph would have been familiar with God's speaking through dreams from Scriptures, how did Joseph know that it was God speaking and not just a nightmare? How do we know when God is speaking to us? *Joseph knew.* I think that today we know. We do not always want to know, and even more, we do not want to act on what we know. Joseph knew, and he acted. He did not decide to go back to sleep and try to remember the dream in the morning or to look for someone to interpret the dream. Joseph acted immediately.

Sometimes when we stop at a rest area, we do so to calm our nerves after having narrowly missed having a car accident. We might realize we made an almost fatal mistake in our driving. We might thank God for saving us from another driver's carelessness. At our Twelve Days of Christmas rest stop, we ask God's forgiveness for sins committed, for things we ought to have done and did not. We give thanks for times that we have avoided tragedy or resisted temptation. We put that old calendar of happiness and sorrow, of success and failure, in the recycle bin. We put up the new calendar of blank pages to fill with new beginnings and opportunities.

We rest for a bit and we dream. To make those dreams come true, we check our maps. In my denomination, we have John Wesley's quadrilateral of Scripture, Experience, Tradition, and Reason serving as road signs. What are your signs? Where are the yield, the caution, and the stop signs? Where are the detours? Joseph took detours and changed his plans. Because of Christmas, we do not have to rely only on our dreams for direction; now we have the gift of Christ, who shows us the way.

After our rest stop of Christmastide, it is time to get back on the road, to head in the direction that allows God to work through us in the New Year. We have opened once again that gift of Love. We do not have to travel alone. God is with us, with each of us.

Prayer: Loving God, we give thanks for the rest stops in our lives. In this time of planning for the New Year, help us to pause to set priorities. Help us to read our maps in whatever form we find those maps. Be with us as we listen, pray, and journey into this New Year. Amen.

Long-Range Plans

Read Genesis 12:1–9 and Matthew 1:23–25.

Like the highway in the middle of the night, the clean lines on the calendar wait for the traffic of days to enter and pass through. Celebrations, committee meetings, and appointments will be noted. Some events will be detoured and many sped through. The days will pass. How do we make the most of the time ahead?

What is worth writing on that new calendar? What is merely clutter and chaos? Planning for group meetings or for our daily schedules requires discernment. Opportunities as well as challenges, strengths as well as weaknesses, and dreams as well as reality are all part of the planning process.

Traveling back through the days and months of the previous year brings tender smiles, laughter, and some tears. The filled calendar is a reflection of my past life. It cannot be changed.

Unexpected insights do catch me by surprise. Some events were more significant than I realized at the time. I had failed to see the whole picture. When we are traveling, I occasionally look in the visor mirror for a quick grooming. The reality of right now literally faces me. Yesterday I was that, and today I am this. I looked younger once; I will look older in the future. When I take my small magnifying mirror from my purse, I find the image too close and personal. I am focused on the magnified imperfections and do not see the whole picture. Planning requires seeing that large picture.

Distance changes the perspective. The rearview mirror outside my car window has this warning: Objects are closer than they appear. The upcoming events noted on my new calendar many times echo that warning. In January, that birthday in April seems far in the future, but it is closer than I think. Distance also provides perspective on the importance of events. What lessons do I find on last year's calendar? What filled spaces should not be repeated? Looking back through the days, how many were blank spaces that enabled rest and renewal?

Where will the days in this new calendar take me? I remember the story of Abraham and Sarah and the many times they left the familiar, went into the unknown, and made drastic changes in their plans. I remember that Abraham and Sarah, even in their old age, were given new life to nurture. I remember that Abraham and Sarah changed even their names. Most of all, I remember that Abraham and Sarah listened to God and traveled in faith. I must do the same.

As Christians, we know that God will be with us. The Holy Spirit will surround us in comfort when we weep because loved ones die. We will feel God's smile when we laugh and play. Children will be born. The seasons will come as surely as the sun rises each morning. In the midst of the unknown, we have the order and beauty of the Lord's earth, which we share for moments or decades. It is good.

I take my pencil (all long-range plans should be written in pencil) and start to write on those pages of time. Stuffing the dates here and leaving some blank there, I start my travel through those new calendar pages.

This is the year the Lord has given. I will rejoice and be glad in it.

Prayer: Creator God, the blank pages of our new calendars are both inspiring and daunting. Guide us as we fill our moments and days. May all that we do and say in this New Year reflect praise, prayer, and lives dedicated to you. Amen.

Lent

With or without an awareness of other seasons in our liturgical calendars, most people are aware of the season of Lent. But beyond giving up chocolate candy or soft drinks, Lent offers the opportunity for real spiritual growth through special Lenten studies and spiritual growth retreats. Lent is an opportunity for self-examination. It is a time for an honest look at our sins, our failures, and our need for grace.

Brown Leaves

Read Romans 5:6–11.

The dry leaves of iris, mums, and feverfew cover the flowerbed. The fall yellows of the redbud and elm leaves are mottled with brown and matted from the winter snows. Beneath this messy mulch, the tender shoots of daffodils, tulips, and hyacinths hold their promise of the brightness of new life. The buds on the lilac bushes are swelling with hints of purple. Spring is sending its invitation to a coming-out party. I want a uniform background for that invitation. The yellows and blues, the whites and lavenders need an uncluttered canvas in time for Easter. I begin to carefully remove the dried material and replace it with finely ground compost.

Fatigue fells the project when only half finished. Gathering the tools and mentally measuring the mound of debris still present, I stop midway to the brush pile.

If I think of this bed as a symbol of new life, of fresh beginnings, if I think of this bed as a symbol of the resurrection, why am I intent on removing all evidence of the old? There was no cleaning up of the bed of deceit, intrigue, and sin before Christ arose. That is precisely the point: Christ came out of the mess as it was. That is what makes his resurrection so powerful. No cleaning up first or grinding the sins into bits that gives an outward appearance of neatness and acceptability. The promise of new life comes from the brown, dry edges, the dirt and the dirges, the slime and sludge of life, as it exists. A cross of death became a symbol for victory over death.

Just as Christ rose above the violence and degradation of that time, the empty cross is above my own heap of the brown leaves of my individual sins and the collective sins of my world. Violence and hunger, injustice and apathy clutter today's world. As much as I might try, I cannot always do those things I want to do. I blame my excessive consumption on the influences of our culture. I rationalize that my one voice cannot influence national policy. The list of the sins of omission and commission is endless. I have a lot of brown leaves in my life.

Yet, Christ comes through it all and shines his promise of life and love and forgiveness to each of us just as surely as the golden daffodils will come through those old leaves and bloom.

The mystery, the promise of Easter, is too much for me to grasp. I do not have to understand all of it. The miracle, the reality of the resurrection is not dependent on my comprehension of that miraculous gift. Someday I will understand more fully. For now, it is enough just to know that Christ conquered sin and death and turned that world and mine upside down.

Prayer: For the symbols all around us of forgiveness and new life, we thank you, Lord. Remind us again of the utterly astounding message of the resurrection. Open our eyes to see the cross above the homely heaps of our lives. Be with us as we come to you even with tasks unfinished. Amen.

Which One Is He?

Read Matthew 16:13–16.

I hurried down the hospital corridor. Nurses smiled knowingly as I rushed past. In front of the nursery window, the row of bundled babies blinked their dark eyes at the bright lights. A robust baby girl with lots of dark hair and sallow skin was at center front. I searched the tiny faces for a miniature reproduction of our fair-skinned blond daughter. Where was my granddaughter?

"Right in front of you," said the nurse.

I was taken aback. This was not what I had envisioned. All of our babies were fair-skinned with wisps of very light hair on their scalps. This baby looked like her father! I was embarrassed and surprised at myself. I did not realize how much I had assumed that our daughter's first child would look like her. This baby was not typical of our family's newborns. I had different expectations. Expectations that I did not realize were there until those expectations were not met.

Jesus was not what the Jewish community expected either. Were they to believe that a baby born to plain people, two nobodies really, could be the Messiah? No royal robes, no fine linen covering against the chill of the night, and worse still, born in a makeshift room at the inn. Then this babe grew strong and wise and in favor with

God. He left his family, which probably included his widowed mother and his siblings, and went out to preach. He walked the countryside, not riding in a chariot with soldiers clearing the way for him as would be proper for a king. This man acted more like a servant than a king. He stirred up trouble in the synagogue. He called the religious hierarchy to account. He hung around with the lower class, ate with sinners, and had smelly fishermen as part of his support group.

Yet, this Jesus did amazing things. He must be someone special. Who was he really? Elijah or Jeremiah, John the Baptist, or some prophet back from the dead?

"What about you?" Jesus asked the disciples. "Who do you say that I am?"

Peter answered correctly. He proclaimed Jesus the Messiah, the Son of the living God.

Would I recognize the Messiah? Would you? When we seriously study the Scriptures, what do we find different about Jesus from what we expected? Whom do you expect? Do I recognize Jesus when I encounter him unexpectedly in my life? Do you?

Prayer: Lord Jesus, we often fail to recognize you in our midst. Secretly we expect you to be at least in distinctive dress or surrounded by some great light. Open our eyes. Wipe away our preconceived images of you. Tear away the blinders from our eyes, and enter into our hearts. We long to know you more fully that we might recognize you in the homes and hallways of our lives. Amen.

Holy Week

Some of us would like to just skip this week that goes from triumph through betrayal and death. Yet, how can we appreciate Easter without remembering what led to Easter? We can't afford to ignore these events. What would we have done? Which characters would we have been in the drama? Which characters are we now?

Do I Know You?

Read Matthew 23:1–12.

If you knocked at Christ's door, would Christ say, "Do I know you?" Imagine yourself listening to Jesus. It is the Tuesday of what we call Holy Week. Jesus is speaking to a crowd just outside the temple. His disciples are with him, and the crowd is full of potential disciples, people who admire and love Jesus and who, at this point, are not afraid to be identified with him. The twelve apostles are still riding high on the triumphal entry and on the welcome given Jesus. They are encouraged by the warm reception from the people. They feel completely loyal to Jesus, proud of their leader and their group.

What Jesus preached after that triumphant entry must have seemed harsh to his disciples. Chapters 23 through 25 in Matthew are full of judgment and warnings. Jesus gave many warnings in our passage of Scripture. The characteristics of the religious people that most troubled him seemed to be that their actions failed to match their words, that they made demands of others that those in charge were unwilling to follow in their own lives, and that they acted for the wrong reasons in order to make a favorable impression.

Jesus talked about titles. We are not certain what Matthew meant by *rabbi* since the term had various meanings at that time, but it seems to mean that in the Christian community, we are all one family and only Jesus deserves the highest title. We know that frequently the pastors in churches, who are called by various titles, are in reality very humble servants. We know that sometimes those Christians who call themselves "just" ministers or "just" pastors or "just" laity are the most arrogant and self-centered, the most obsessed with power. Words can be used to deceive. Although titles can be useful as proof of authority, these passages from Matthew remind us that titles do not make us somehow closer to God. Titles are meaningless to God. We are all "just"—yet wonderfully, majestically—children of God, all brothers and sisters in Christ.

This sermon makes us uncomfortable. We can see ourselves as members of that unworthy crowd.

Now imagine that you are in a reception line to meet the Master. As you move closer to Christ, you wish that you had brought a list of all the committees you have led, of all the places where you are listed as a major contributor. You wish that you had worn your choir robe. When finally you are face to face with Christ, he looks puzzled and says, "Do I know you?"

But, fortunately, we know that the story does not end with the palm waving or with the warnings, but with the resurrection and reconciliation. We are an Easter people.

Imagine another reception line. As you get closer and

closer to Christ, you realize that your masks won't work, your lists of good deeds are too short and the motives not always pure; you are unworthy, certainly not good enough to meet the Master. You feel like an impostor in this line. You wonder if you can slip out of the line to come back another time to another line when you are ready, but it is too late. Jesus has seen you. You are filled with mixtures of hope and fear, joy and terror. You think to yourself, *Only by the grace of God will I be able to go forward.*

Then Jesus says to you, "I know you. You are already forgiven and loved. Come with me."

Prayer: God of love, we relate easily to the triumphant entry, the loud praises, and the optimism of the Palm Sunday events. We like choirs in splendid robes and dignitaries passing before us. We are proud of our titles. Let us hear your words and remember that those titles and splendid robes mean nothing in your eyes. We are an Easter people, each one of us a known and beloved child. As your children, we humbly ask your blessing. Amen.

Company in the Garden

Read John 18:1–9.

Jesus and his disciples frequently went to a quiet garden across the Kidron Valley. We assume that this garden was a place of retreat for them. Jesus and the eleven disciples were in this garden that evening when Judas betrayed Jesus.

Did the disciples have any idea of what was going to happen? Jesus had tried to tell them repeatedly of what was to come, but they failed to grasp the meaning of his words. Perhaps they were afraid. Perhaps they did not want to believe that Jesus' time on earth was about to end.

After the hours Jesus spent in agonizing prayer, after the long vigil when the disciples failed to stay awake and keep watch, Judas came with soldiers and police from the chief priests and Pharisees to arrest Jesus. The group carried lanterns, torches, and weapons. It must have been quite a crowd. Judas stood with the soldiers, not with the disciples. We would probably say that he was "trying to save his skin." What sort of resistance were the soldiers expecting?

But Jesus did not offer resistance. He identified himself by saying, "I am he." This answer sounds simple enough to us, but to the soldiers it was a powerful statement with deeper meaning. By saying the words "I am," Jesus meant that he is what God is. The soldiers fell to the ground, in response to the manifestation of God. They acknowledged, at least for those moments, the power and presence of God. When the arrest procedure continued, Jesus asked that the disciples be let go. Judas need not have worried about guilt by association after all. The Good Shepherd takes care of his sheep.

Although the soldiers and police were armed, expecting resistance, Jesus took charge of the situation. Identifying himself as the one they were seeking, he asked that his disciples not be taken and went quietly with the soldiers. Their weapons were unnecessary. Jesus, not the soldiers, was in charge.

Jesus had the company of his disciples in the garden. We assume that the disciples did not expect additional company, especially Judas, who had disappeared from the table. Can you imagine the disciples' terror when Judas suddenly appeared with soldiers and police? Judas knew the way to the garden. His feet had been washed and his hunger fed by Jesus. He was a part of the inner circle. In his betrayal of Jesus, Judas led evil into the garden.

That is hard for us to understand. We would like to make sense of this event, to make some sort of excuse for Judas. Maybe he needed the money to help his family or friends; maybe he was saving money for some emergency. We do not like to think that someone who had been close to Jesus would betray him for money. The Gospel of John doesn't make excuses. The account seems stark.

I think the account is horrifying to us in part because we know that we too sometimes put money—"just this once, just this once"—ahead of living faithfully. We would like to think that our little lapses are not at all like bringing betrayal or guiding evil company into the garden. Except that little lapses become a pattern. Betrayal takes many forms and becomes easier and easier. We also know that our betrayal of Jesus might come in some significant, consciously made decision; others have known light, love, and life and yet chosen darkness, evil, and death.

This account of company in the garden is frightening stuff. Jesus had company in the garden—the company of his faithful disciples, who stood a sleepy watch, and the company of the one who betrayed him by coming with police and soldiers.

Which company are you?

Prayer: O God, sometimes we feel like the disciples in the garden. We too would like to keep a faithful watch but find ourselves sleeping. Circumstances overwhelm us, and we fail to respond. Forgive our lack of attention to your commands. Enable us, even with our mortal weaknesses, to keep awake in the garden. Forgive us, we pray, for the times we have betrayed you by inaction or by selfish choices. Amen.

Three Strikes

Read John 18:15–17, 25–27.

"Strike three—you're out!"

Shoulders slumped, head bowed, my little friend shuffled from the field. I could sense his utter discouragement. He had promised his teammates that this time he would be the one to hit the home run to win the game. He had tried hard. Three times, he had swung the bat with all his might and yet missed the ball. Would they forgive him if they lost this game? Would he ever have the courage to be at bat again?

From neighborhood baseball games in vacant lots to major-league games in huge stadiums, the rules are the same—three strikes and you're out. We carry those rules with us into our workplaces and even into our homes. Three strikes or three mistakes—just three failures—and we are out of the game, out of a job, or at the very least in the time-out corner. We know the rules. Patience has limits. Goals must be met. Allowing three chances seems generous. The rules of the game are unwavering.

We might not be able to imagine ourselves betraying Jesus as Judas did, but the story of Peter's denials is altogether different. We can sympathize with Peter. We know our own limits all too well. We know the temptation to put our own well-being ahead of our discipleship. Longing to be accepted and approved by our friends and family often drives us to denial. We sometimes remain silent rather than take the risks involved in confronting injustice to our neighbors. We prefer to conform, to keep our lives running smoothly. We have many traveling companions on the road to wealth and fame.

We might marvel that Peter denied Jesus only three times. Peter's denials are no surprise. Like some of us, Peter spoke and acted on impulse. He made hasty promises that he could not keep. Peter was very human.

We, too, are human. We struggle to forgive our friends who make false accusations against us or betray our confidence. Our hearts are broken when our friends deny us. Yet, rather than stand firm in the face of danger, we deny our friends. Only a great love can save us from ourselves.

But three strikes did not put Peter out. Peter's limited love and our limited love are in sharp contrast to the limitless love of Jesus. The Gospels do not record that Jesus rebuked Peter for his denials. The story just goes on because the story is primarily about Jesus, not about Peter. Jesus expresses his love by laying down his life for his friends, even for Peter and even for us.

Prayer: Dear God, reading about the events of Holy Week is difficult for us. We do not want to deny Christ. Yet, sometimes we are afraid. Sometimes we deny you by our actions or by our silence. We do not deserve the incredible generosity of your grace. Oh, grant us that grace. Amen.

Who Is Worthy?

Read Romans 5:6–11.

Before our first child was born, I thought that I knew about love. I had grown up a loved child and sister. I have a loving husband. The love that enveloped me as I looked at our firstborn was different and totally overwhelming. I knew that I would give all I possessed for his health and happiness. I would protect my child with all my strength. I would even give my life for him. The miracle of that love was repeated with each child. Love was not divided, but multiplied. Most parents feel this way about their children.

Our Scripture says that God's love for his children is even greater. The example given of this love is Christ's dying for us while we are still sinners. Hard stuff this Scripture. There is no question that I would risk my life to save my husband, our children, a sibling, and close relatives. We had foster children and exchange students whom we loved. I like to think I would give my life for one of those children. If someone like Mother Teresa were in peril, I would help without thinking of my own safety. I think I would save anyone that I could.

Yet, would I risk my life for a bag lady? I think so. Would it be appropriate for me to dash into the street to push a thief or a gang member out of the way of an approaching truck? Would they be worth it? Who is worthy? What if I were the sole caretaker for someone else who needed me? How far am I supposed to go in imitating Christ?

Christ died for us while we were yet sinners, still unworthy. What does that example of self-sacrifice mean for me as I make my decisions? In reality, I have never had to answer that question. I have not had to risk my life to save the life of another. Not much has been demanded of me.

Or has it? Have I been blind to the opportunities for sacrificial living and giving? Each time I decide which appeal for funds for refugees or starving children or women in poverty to support with a donation, I am making a decision about whom or what effort is worthy. How many times have I subconsciously judged someone by his or her appearance? How many times have I dismissed an opinion because I did not consider it worth my attention? Could self-sacrifice also mean letting others have the credit for an idea? Could it mean postponing or giving up my dream to enable someone else to fulfill a dream? Could it mean allowing others to use their talents while I take back stage? Those examples seem too small, too easy in comparison to the example of Christ.

I feel unworthy. Yet, through Christ I know that we are all worthy. Believing the unbelievable gift of grace, is there anyone that I would not risk my life to save?

Prayer: Dear God of grace, thank you for your gift of love and reconciliation, which is almost too much for us to grasp. We can never deserve it. We will never be worthy. Only by your grace, only by your grace. Amen.

Easter

"We are an Easter people," one of our pastors frequently reminded us. And we need reminding because for many of us Easter is sunrise services, hearing *The Messiah* sung once again, and an Easter brunch after services. But Easter is never really over. Death is conquered. The resurrection continues.

Lockdown

Read John 20:19–31.

It was midnight. Our house was dark and empty, the doors securely locked. Getting inside required considerable ingenuity on the part of our daughter Joan. In accordance with school policy, she had come home from the state track meet on the school bus while we drove home in our car. Unfortunately, she had arrived home before us. Joan slipped into the space between the large evergreen shrubs and her bedroom window. After several attempts, she had opened the window wide enough that she could slip safely into her room. When we arrived, we were surprised to see her already home and in the house.

Decades ago most residential doors in our town were left unlocked, and Joan would have had no trouble just walking in the front door. As in most small rural communities at that time, the trust level was very high. The dangers came not from thieves but from fickle weather and uncertain prices for crops. Now the population has increased, and an interstate highway skirts the city limits. Attitudes have changed. Now we regularly lock our doors. Even though we have never had any real reason to be afraid, locked doors give us a sense of security.

In the days following the crucifixion, the disciples did have reason to be afraid and to lock the door. The One whom they had followed had been tried, found guilty, and crucified. They feared the consequences of guilt by association. Slipping quietly through the evening shadows, they crept into their meeting room and quickly locked the door behind them. As they huddled together in prayer and fear, did they wonder if they would be next on the authorities' hit list? Who knew their names? Who had seen them with Jesus?

They feared not only their enemies, but also their God. They had fled, and they had denied Jesus. They knew that one of them had blatantly betrayed Jesus. Were they also guilty of betrayal? They had not helped Jesus carry the cross. Not one of them had defied the crowd's hateful taunts. Now, even with the door locked, they were afraid.

Then the incredible, unanticipated thing happened—Jesus came into the room in spite of the locked door. He made his first appearance after the crucifixion to this group of disciples. Had some of the group begun to doubt his promise to them that they would see him again? We can only imagine their joy when he came to them. How relieved the group must have been when they heard him say, "Peace be with you." Christ came to the disciples with compassion and grace. No scolding for running away and hiding. No demand for confession of misdeeds. Christ came to them through the locked door and wished them peace.

That spring evening Joan came into our home in spite of locked doors. We had not intended to lock her out, but sometimes we do purposely attempt to lock out Christ. This Easter some of us have locked ourselves in our spiritual rooms and gardens. We quake in our solitary cells, ashamed of our sins and of our failures. We are unworthy. We too have doubted and denied Christ by word and deed. We are afraid Christ might come in the darkness and enter the locked doors to our hearts. We know our sins only too well, even if our friends and family do not. We know that God knows. And we are afraid. Maybe, if we lock the door, we will have time to get our lives in order before Christ comes.

Then Christ comes through the locked door. Christ comes to us and dispels our unbelief by whatever means we need. We cannot lock out Christ even if we try.

Prayer: Loving, patient, and persistent God, like a parent you come to us even as we hold our hands over our ears to shut out your words. You come to us when we try to hide. You come to us when we lock our doors in fear. Thank you, thank you, Lord. Amen.

Pentecost

Several years ago our congregation celebrated Pentecost by having the account in Acts 2:1–13 read in the native languages of the different nationalities represented in our congregation. It was a deeply moving experience and a reminder that the Holy Spirit comes to each of us in a way we understand. At this writing, we are having one of those windy days common in our area with gusts over sixty miles an hour. It is not one of my favorite weather events. I wonder how frightened the people were by that "violent wind" mentioned in Acts.

The Wind

Read Acts 2:1–13.

My childhood home at Cedar Row, a farm in northeast Kansas, is nestled against a hill where cedars provide protection from winter winds and elms offer shade from summer heat. The windswept wheat field in northwest Kansas that my husband and I were considering as our future home site was very different. There was no protection from the wind, only sky and wheat, not even a farmhouse in view. Although my husband loves these open spaces, the immense sky, and even the wind, I tearfully asked him to consider another option. As a compromise, with the wind as one of our considerations, we chose a site in a new development at the edge of Colby and built our home. We planted trees, including seedlings from Cedar Row. Now, I too love this area with its open spaces, low humidity, and cool nights.

The wind and I have a more tenuous relationship. I still find very windy days unpleasant. Like everyone in our part of the country, I know about wind. Contrary to popular myth, Kansas does not lead the nation in tornadoes, but many of our communities have heard the roar of tornadoes and suffered the subsequent damage. The roar of the violent wind of a tornado is heard by everyone in its path. We respect the power of the wind.

The crowd at Pentecost must have experienced something that was literally soulshaking. It was described as a violent wind. Did they huddle together in awe and fear or scatter looking for shelter? Wind-whipped tongues, like tongues of fire, descended on each person. The people began to speak in other languages.

The message was given in many languages so that each person present, even those from far away, could understand. Yet, the whole experience was beyond understanding. No mere words could describe the experience. The Holy Spirit came like a violent wind and like tongues of fire. And it came to everyone present. Everyone. Inclusive.

Although we claim to be inclusive in our faith communities, our actions often speak otherwise. Sanctuaries with traditional pews and classical organ music can be exclusive. Sanctuaries with movable folding chairs, the latest sound systems, and electronic music can also be exclusive. Yet, both are filled with people who share much in language, in social standards, and in faith. Even with this commonality, misunderstandings and claims of spiritual superiority can arise. Some might claim a special, exclusive experience of the Holy Spirit.

Reading Luke's story of Pentecost again, we are reminded that the Holy Spirit is not the private property of any one of us. Pentecost was a *group* experience. Everyone and anyone who believes can receive the Holy Spirit, with or without our prior approval. The Holy Spirit fell on the whole crowd there, and it can fall on crowds (congregations) here today.

Watch out for tongues of fire. Every lip touched by the heat of that fire can proclaim the Gospel in its own unique language. Listen for the roar of the wind. It might be a noisy time with everyone talking at once and persons with different viewpoints suddenly understanding each other. It might mean things happen that are beyond our imaginations. It might mean things happen that could only take place when the wind of the Holy Spirit sweeps us off our feet and sends us sailing.

Prayer: Almighty God, descend on our assemblies today. Blow away our distrust and prejudices. Scour the practice of assumed privilege from us as the wind scours the earth with its mighty roar. Give us new breath to proclaim your love. Let us hear your voice in our own tongues that we might speak to others in words we can all understand. Forgive us our reluctance. We are afraid of strong winds. Give us courage and be with us as we are carried in new directions by the Holy Spirit. Amen.

Ordinary Time

I have always preferred the term Ordinary Time to Kingdomtide. To me it is a reminder that Ordinary Time is where we live most of our lives. Ordinary time can also be a holy time. I enjoy celebrations, but most of my days I am quite content to rejoice in the ordinary pleasures of sunrises and sunsets, of birds and squirrels in the backyard trees, of simple meals and quiet talk with family and friends. I expect extraordinary experiences at Christmas and Easter, but extraordinary events can and do happen in the ordinary periods of my life. Those extraordinary events are appreciated even more because they occur in the middle of the ordinary.

Ordinary Time:
A Responsive Reading

Read Luke 18:18–30.

When I was a young child, I did not memorize the alphabet in order as children do today. When I began to use the dictionaries and encyclopedias, I found it necessary to organize all of those wonderful letters. It seemed to me that the letters were in the wrong sequence. Why isn't Q at the end of the alphabet with all of the other seldom used letters like X and Z?

It comes as no surprise then that as an adult I have wondered why Christmas and Easter are so close together on our calendars. If those two Christian holy days were further apart, it would certainly help to balance worship attendance and offerings through the year. Further spacing would give church choir leaders, clergy, and the rest of us more time to focus on Lent instead of going so quickly from Christmas cantatas to Easter anthems.

Of course, there is the possibility that the church fathers had it right. Officially, the Christian year is divided into two cycles: the Christmas cycle including Advent/Christmas/Epiphany and the Easter cycle including Lent/Easter/Pentecost. Each division includes times of preparation, celebration, and growth. The growth periods are commonly called Ordinary Time. The time for growth following the

Christmas season is relatively short. The long Ordinary Time following Pentecost is often called Kingdomtide. Your church worship bulletin may simply indicate the number of Sundays after Pentecost. Whatever designation is given those weeks, most laity pay little attention. They have recognized Advent and Lent and celebrated Christmas and Easter. The weeks following Pentecost are a time for family vacations, fewer church meetings, and an excuse to worship by a lake or a ball diamond. For those who stay at home, Ordinary Time becomes either a season of bland worship with substitute pastors or a welcome vacation from frantic church activity, depending on their perspective.

I have begun to think of this longer Ordinary Time as a living responsive reading to the joy and reflection of the other church seasons. The freedom from frantic church schedules during those many weeks gives an opportunity to absorb and live the meaning of the parables and of the events in the life of Christ. The parables are primarily lived out on the ordinary plains of our lives, not in the valleys or on the mountaintops. How many vacation days are needed to trudge across that vast plain of Ordinary Time, to go from judgment to justice, to respond to the pleas for forgiveness of the thief and the murderer? How many weeks do I need to absorb the awesome reality of the Holy Spirit with us always? To establish the discipline of daily prayer and Scripture reading that is longer than fifteen minutes? To respond to the least of these, near and far away? To respond to all the other commands of Christ?

I might encounter parched places on this ordinary plain. I may stumble on stones of rejection and discouragement. I know I will find pools of clean water and rest in the shade. Because of the mountaintops of Christmas and Easter, I know that God is always with me.

How does my life read as a response to the gift of Christmas, the sacrifice of Good Friday, the triumph of Easter? Am I listening to the different tongues of Pentecost? My Ordinary Time responsive reading might go like this:

Leader: When God chose them, Zechariah and
    Elizabeth were very old, but Mary was very young.
*Response: We are never too young and we are never
    too old to be chosen by God.*

Leader: Shepherds and wise men were told of Christ's
    birth.
*Response: Whether we are rich or poor or somewhere
    in between, God may speak to us.*

Leader: Jesus attended synagogue, as was his custom.
*Response: No matter how righteous we may be, we
    still need corporate worship.*

Leader: Jesus chose ordinary people to be his apostles.
Response: God can use each one of us.

Leader: Jesus withdrew from the crowds to pray.
Response: No job is more important than regular time with God.

Leader: Jesus taught and healed all kinds of people.
Response: No criteria must be met for entrance through the church doors.

Leader: The lives of the Apostles and all those touched by Jesus were changed dramatically.
Response: As disciples, we must expect and accept change and be willing to accept the change in others.

Leader: Jesus said, "Follow me."
Response: Discipleship has no time limits. It is for a lifetime, not just a few weeks or months.

Leader: The Holy Spirit came upon a crowd.
Response: Pentecost was not an individual matter. People who speak a language different from our own share equally with us in the gift of Pentecost.

I have neither enough pages to write an adequate responsive reading for Ordinary Time nor enough days in Ordinary Time to give sufficient response to the wonders and gifts of the other seasons.

Ordinary Time: A Responsive Reading

Prayer: O Lord, our Teacher, Redeemer, and Comforter, take our lives that we might truly live. Grant us the patience and persistence to take full advantage of our ordinary days, and make those days a joyous response to your love. Amen.

Come and See

Read John 1:29–51.

Several years ago, we hiked down the trail into the Grand Canyon with our family of six, our exchange student, and two of her friends from New Zealand. The colorful layers of rock and clay spread before us like illustrations in a geological textbook. The ages of the earth stacked one upon the other formed steep walls alongside the trails.

Hiking in groups of two or three, we began our trek down the trail, each group at its own pace. At times, just staying on the trail took all of our energy and concentration. At other times, we felt the cool breezes and smelled the scrub pines. We scanned the sweeping panorama and wondered at the vastness around us.

"Look!" we would exclaim as a new scene caught our attention.

"Come and see this!" we called as we urged our companions to our own vantage points.

As the sun cast shadows from distant cliffs and rocks, each group saw the trail at different times in various angles of light. Some of us clung to shrubs on narrow paths to let burros pass, while others on wider parts of the trail stepped aside for the burros. Some saw wildlife and some did not. We all relaxed together by the cooling stream at the bottom of the canyon.

Those miniature scenes from the trail and the large canvas from the rim could be put together in a beautiful collage, but even that picture could not capture the total splendor of the canyon. The views were both too small and too large for us to grasp. Nine hikers had nine different perspectives. And each was true. Yet, no one experience gave the total picture.

In this Scripture, John the Baptizer invites us to "look," and Jesus invites us to "come and see." In this one marvelous chapter, we see many different snapshots of God put together in a great collage. Jesus is named as Lamb of God who takes away the sin of the world, Son of God, Lamb of God, Rabbi (which translated means Teacher), the Messiah (which translated means Anointed), he about whom Moses in the law and also the prophets wrote, Son of Joseph from Nazareth, King of Israel, and Son of Man.

So many names! None of the titles given in this chapter of John encompasses a complete picture of Jesus. The titles are only the beginning. Someday we will see the greater picture.

From the rim of the canyon, we could not fully appreciate all its aspects. We had to go down the trail, take the many switchbacks, cling to bushes along the way, and refresh ourselves at the stream at the bottom before we resumed our hiking. Our faith journeys are much like that trip down the trail at the Grand Canyon. We might long to linger, warm and safe, on the rim. Sooner or later—either by choice or by surprise—straining for a closer look, we will tumble onto the trail and into the big picture. At times, the most we will manage is to hang on to some support while others pass on the trail. At other times, we have at least a glimpse of the whole beautiful picture of life. At each turn of the trail, Christ will be revealed in more detail.

"Look!" we will say to our trail companions.

And we will hear Christ say, "Come and see."

Prayer: O God, our Creator and Creator of the plains and canyons where we live and look, pray and play, we thank you for the simple things in our lives that remind us of the vastness of your love and care. Help us to recognize the wonder of your Being, so that we might say to others, "Look!" and hear you say, "Come and see!" Amen.

But Wait—There's More!

Read Luke 4:14–30.

"But wait—there's more! Take advantage of our offer now, and we have even more wonderful products to offer you for this one low price. Act now! The supply is limited."

The announcer had been droning on, repeating amazing claims about the virtues of his fantastic product. But I was not amazed. His message was familiar. I had heard this spiel before. My thoughts wandered to dinner plans, letters to write, calls to make, and the weather forecast. As I searched for the remote control, his excitement suddenly blared at me from the television, loud enough to be heard in the next room over running water. He must have guessed that my attention would be wandering by now to chores awaiting me in the kitchen.

"But wait—there's more," he said in a more measured tone. "Let me tell you about all the things I can do with this great product." He was a smooth-talking young man, but I was not convinced. My kitchen tool drawer was full of utensils that worked just fine for my style of cooking.

"But wait—there's more!" he said again. And his claims became more and more extravagant. This was getting ridiculous. Who would believe all that? His claims were outrageous. Nothing works that way in the real world. Whatever the offer, there's always more, if only we will keep listening and take advantage of the next exciting offer. I was through listening.

"But wait—" I finally found the remote control. Maybe I would miss something important, but I certainly didn't think so. With a swift click, I banished that man from my family room and went on with my satisfactory life. But he just kept on talking, broadcast into countless other homes where other people might get the message, believe it, act on it, and take advantage of his offer.

"But wait—there's more!" I seem to hear Jesus saying to me as I read this passage from Luke. There *is* more, and the more makes me uncomfortable. Jesus had come out of the wilderness and the temptation experience. He went to Galilee, where he taught in the synagogues and was praised by the people. In the synagogue in Nazareth, he read from a scroll the words of Isaiah, words very familiar to all of the people listening. They had heard these prophecies read countless times before. Did their thoughts jump ahead to activities they had planned for the remainder of the Sabbath?

"But wait—there's more!" Jesus was telling the people in the synagogue that day. After he finished the reading, Jesus announced that he is the one the Scripture is talking about! The Scripture was fulfilled that day. The worshipers suddenly realized that there was more to this reading and commentary than they were accustomed to hearing. This teacher Jesus was making some amazing claims. What was he saying? What was happening on this ordinary Sabbath?

But wait—there's more. Jesus went public and made himself known, not only as the son of Joseph the carpenter, who had raised him in this little village, but also—and this is the amazing part—*as the Son of God.* Jesus gave his inaugural address that day. Jesus claimed his authority and proclaimed the theme for his ministry.

But not all of the people listening that day in the synagogue got the message. Many heard what they expected and wanted to hear. Some thought that he was a wonderful person. "Just think!" they seemed to say. "This is a hometown boy! Who would have thought it? And he speaks so well! He seems so wise!"

But wait—there's more. Some of the people understood that what Jesus was saying to them was not just the words they already knew. Jesus had added something to the reading. This was the new world order. This was a new paradigm. Things were changing. Listen, really listen, to the Scripture. Believe it. The ancient vision of loving care for those at the edges of society was really going to happen. And that thought was scary indeed for those who took pride in their faith heritage, who were secure in their places of privilege. Hadn't they earned that privilege by observing the Sabbath and the Law?

A murmur spread through the synagogue. There was more to this message, they realized, than they wanted to hear. Just as I didn't want that hawker telling me to change my way of cooking, the people of Nazareth didn't want Jesus telling them to change their comfortable lives. If what Jesus said were true, not only privilege but also selfish excesses and lavish comforts were going to have to go. Foreigners, people that they did not want to associate with or even to touch, were going to be blessed and would share in God's love and grace! What sort of sermon was this? They were offended and angry. When I was through listening, I simply clicked the remote control button; but these people escorted Jesus, their hometown prophet and the Son of God, out of town.

Some say that we have not really heard the gospel message until that message makes us angry or at least uncomfortable. At that moment, we begin to really hear the gospel. It is then that we find our lives transformed.

I wonder how I would have reacted if I had been in that synagogue long ago? Would I have had to change my views of my community? Would my status in that community have been threatened? Today there is no doubt that, in the world's view, I am among the privileged. I am a part of my culture and share in both the sins and the righteousness of my community and of my church. Is my present status threatened by these words of Jesus?

How would you have reacted if you had heard Jesus reading and teaching in the synagogue that day? Would you have listened for more? How do we determine which of our cultural values conform to the values of Christ and which values need to be discarded? The difference can be difficult to distinguish. It can be even more difficult to act on our awareness of the difference.

But wait—there's more. There is always more to experience and to understand. There was more revelation of Scripture that day in the synagogue than the people had anticipated. When we read the Scriptures, too often we do a little editing here and there. Sometimes the verses are so familiar that we fail to see the deeper meaning. We ignore or tone down those claims that might call for radical changes in lifestyle or relationships. Today we see and understand only dimly. Read the Scriptures again. What is your reaction? Is there more?

Prayer: O Christ, open our ears that we may hear the whole message. Open our minds that we may understand the depth of meaning in your message. And give us the courage to live what we understand. Amen.

Sending Forth:

John Pratt's Granary

Read Psalm 19:1.

Sunsets are awe-inspiring here on the plains, and Dad Horlacher especially appreciated them. Living in the heart of our small town allowed my father-in-law an acceptable view of the evening wonders, but he longed for a wider perspective. His daily ritual of putting the car in the garage in the early evening offered him the opportunity for that enhanced view. Often, instead of driving the car from the parking area in front of the house, down the alley, and into his garage, he headed for the highway running north out of town.

In the open country, Dad Horlacher would pass fields of wheat and acres of native buffalo grass. Their muted shades of gold and green anchored the crayon colors spilling across the western sky to the distant purple horizon. Free from obstructions of trees and buildings, a panorama of orange, red, and indigo streaked the sky. The sun dropped below the horizon, stretching a violet haze around the northern and southern edges of the earth's rim.

As the brilliant colors of sunset melted into the soft silver-blue shadows of evening, John Pratt's granary came into view. The large, boxy, gray metal granary sat alone on the corner of a country road that met the highway about three miles north of town. The driveway of the granary provided a safe, convenient place for turning around. The heavens had once again proclaimed God's glory. This evening affirmation of God's order and splendor provided a sense of peace and completion to the day for Dad Horlacher. He would return to town and the garage, maybe a little late for supper.

The phrase "by the way of John Pratt's granary" became our family's expression for the long way home, whether across town or across the state. Those extended routes have enabled us to experience beauty that, in our fast-paced lives, we otherwise might have ignored. Taking the time to experience God in the world around us often means going by an alternate route or simply pausing along the way. Some detours reveal God in what we may have considered drab settings, in unexpected encounters with opportunities for service, or in places where we are the recipients of love in action. Wherever we go, God is with us.

I hope that through reading and sharing these meditations you have been enabled to see God in the everyday moments of your life. I pray that you may take the time to go deeper into the ordinary and grow in your relationship with God as you travel "by the way of John Pratt's granary" through your own seasons of salt.

May God bless you,
Millie Horlacher

Sending Forth

May the road rise to meet you,
May the wind be always at your back,
May the sun shine warm upon your face,
May the rains fall soft upon your fields,
And until we meet again,
May God hold you in the palm of his hand.

Amen.

Traditional Gaelic Blessing

About the Author

Millie Hundley Horlacher is a salt-seasoned woman who has more dishrags than dishcloths in her kitchen drawer. She is a certified lay speaker in the United Methodist Church. She has served as Spiritual Growth Coordinator for United Methodist Women on the local, district, and conference levels. Millie is a member of the Board of Trustees of Camp Lakeside United Methodist Center and the district task force for lay speaker schools. She has served on many other church boards, task forces, and committees. Millie's ecumenical activities include Church Women United, World Day of Prayer, and lay speaking in area churches and at statewide gatherings.

Millie was born in Horton, Kansas, in 1933, and was baptized in the Horton Methodist Church. Her happy childhood on the family farm was shared with seven siblings. She attended New Malden one-room rural school, Atchison County Community High School in Effingham, and Kansas State College. She and her husband Wayne live in Colby, Kansas, where they are involved in church and community activities. They have three living children and five grandchildren. Over a dozen foster children and several exchange students have shared their home and their love.

Millie Horlacher's prose and poetry have appeared in *Capper's, Kansas Territorial, Our Way With Words: Kansas Authors Club Centennial Celebration Edition,* and in Christian publications, including *Alive Now.*

CPSIA information can be obtained at www.ICGtesting.com
Printed in the USA
LVOW060622150512

281698LV00003B/2/P